A Book of Consolations

A BOOK OF CONSOLATIONS

SELECTED BY
P. J. Kavanagh

HarperCollins*Publishers*

HarperCollins *Publishers*,
77–85 Fulham Palace Road,
Hammersmith, London w6 8jb

Published by HarperCollins *Publishers* 1992

9 8 7 6 5 4 3 2 1

A catalogue record for this book is
available from the British Library

ISBN 0 00 215969 4

Photoset in Linotron Baskerville by
Rowland Phototypesetting Limited, Bury St Edmunds, Suffolk

Printed in Great Britain by
HarperCollins Manufacturing, Glasgow

WITH THANKS TO KATE

Contents

Acknowledgements

We are grateful to the following authors, owners of copyright, publishers and literary agents who have kindly given permission for poems and passages of prose to appear:

Bloomsbury Publishing Ltd for extracts from *End of a Journey* by Philip Toynbee; Brandt & Brandt Inc for extract from *The Ides of March* by Thornton Wilder; Carcanet Press for lines from 'Judgement Day' by E. J. Scovell; Constable Publishers and Alfred A. Knopf for the poem 'On Being Sixty' from *170 Chinese Poems* by Arthur Waley; Dover Publishing Inc for extracts from *Del Sentimiento Tràgico de la Vida* by Miguel de Unamuno translated by J. E. Crawford Flitch; Faber & Faber Ltd for extracts from *A Grief Observed* by C. S. Lewis, 'The Good Man in Hell' from *Collected Poems* by Edwin Muir, 'Prayer for his mother to say to the Virgin' by Francois Villon translated in *Imitations* by Robert Lowell, 'The Truisms' from *Collected Poems* by Louis MacNeice; Eric Glass Ltd and the Estate of Romola Nijinsky for extract from *Diary* by Vaslav Nijinsky translated by Romola Nijinsky; Grove Weidenfeld for extracts from *Tropic of Cancer* by Henry Miller; Hamish Hamilton Ltd for extracts from *The Unquiet Grave* by Cyril Connolly; William Heinemann Ltd for extracts from *The Colossus of Maroussi* by Henry Miller; David Higham Associates for extract from *Blessings, Kicks and Curses* by Geoffrey Grigson; The Goldsmith Press for 'The Hospital' and 'Epic' by Patrick Kavanagh from *The Complete Poems of Patrick Kavanagh* edited by Peter Kavanagh; North Point Press for *The Book of Job* translated by Stephen Mitchell; Oxford University Press for 'Yesterday Lost', 'Had I a Song' and 'The Escape' from *Collected Poems of Ivor Gurney* edited by P. J. Kavanagh; Oxford University Press (NY) for 'Welsh Incident' in *Collected Poems* by Robert Graves; Pantheon Books Inc for extract from *Dying We Live* by Helmut Gollwitzer and Reinhold Schneider; Penguin Books Ltd for extracts from *Tao Te Ching* by Lao Tzu translated by D. C. Lau, *Letters from a Stoic* by Seneca translated by Robin Campbell, *Meditations* by Marcus Aurelius translated by Maxwell Staniforth; Peters, Fraser & Dunlop for extract from *Heretics* by G. K. Chesterton; Laurence Pollinger Ltd for extracts from *Autobiography* by John

Cowper Powys, *Glory of Life* by Llewelyn Powys; Princeton University Press for extract from *Alchemical Studies* by Carl Gustav Jung; Random Century and the Estate of J. B. Leishman for lines from *Poems* by R. M. Rilke translated by J. B. Leishman; Random Century and the Estate of Virginia Woolf for extracts from *Moments of Being* by Virginia Woolf edited by J. Schulkind; Random Century, Sigmund Freud Copyrights and the Institute of Psycho-Analysis for extract from *The Standard Edition of the Complete Psychological Works of Sigmund Freud* translated and edited by James Strachey; Random Century and the Bodley Head for extract from *The Unquiet Grave* by Cyril Connolly; Rogers, Coleridge & White for extracts from *The Unquiet Grave* by Cyril Connolly; Routledge Ltd for extract from *Collected Works of C. G. Jung*, extracts from *Waiting on God* and *Notebooks* by Simone Weil translated by Emma Cranford; Scolar Press for extracts from *Commonplace Book* by E. M. Forster edited by Philip Gardner; Martin Secker and Warburg for extract from *Herzog* by Saul Bellow, extract from *The Correspondence of Boris Pasternak and Olga Freidenberg 1910–1954*, compiled and edited by Elliot Mossman, translated by Elliot Mossman and Margaret Wettlin, the poem 'Entering My Eightieth Year' from *Persephone's Flowers* by Geoffrey Grigson.

Every effort has been made to contact the copyright owners of material included in this anthology. In the instances where this has not proved possible, we offer our apologies to those concerned.

Introduction

Every generation seeks to console itself as best it can; for doubt, pain, mortality. This search is inevitably, however obliquely, expressed in its literature, and the next generation, smelling complacence, seeks to destroy what it believes to have become false in that consolation, to the dismay of its elders. Thomas Love Peacock tilts at the 'moderns' of his day (1818) in this exchange from *Nightmare Abbey*:

> THE HONOURABLE MR LISTLESS: Sir, I reverence you. But I must say modern books are very consolatory and congenial to my feelings. There is, as it were, a delightful north-east wind, an intellectual blight breathing through them; a delicious misanthropy and discontent, that puts me in a good humour with myself and my sofa.
> MR FLOSKY: Very true, sir. Modern literature is a north-east wind – a blight of the human soul. I take credit to myself for having made it so. The way to produce fine fruit is to blight the flower. You call this a paradox. Marry, so be it. Ponder thereon.

It could be said that here Peacock is consoling himself with exasperated parody. He must have felt better after writing that, and we are cheered that he wrote it.

'Cheered', is that what we mean by 'consolation'? Partly, but there is a sense in which all great literature consoles, therefore cheers, however miserable it may seem to be, because we realize that others have endured our pain, and have laboured to express it. The early nineteenth-century poet Leopardi put at its starkest the idea that Flosky and Listless have taken up as a fashion, have misunderstood, and therefore made absurd:

> Works of genius have this intrinsic property, that even when they give a perfect likeness of the nullity of things, even when

they clearly demonstrate and make us feel the inevitable unhappiness of life, even when they express the most terrible despair,
nevertheless to a great soul, that may find itself in a state of utter
prostration, disillusionment, futility, boredom, and discouragement with life . . . they always serve as a consolation, rekindling
enthusiasm.

We are not all 'great souls' as often as we would like to be, but
'rekindling enthusiasm' is very close to the yardstick used for
this book. The reader is referred to those words of Leopardi (all
those words), if puzzled as to how on earth something chosen
here could ever be consoling. Anger, frustration, despair, defiance (a section is devoted to that), lament (another section –
the consolation of being inconsolable), all these can 'animate'
(to replace Leopardi's words with Matthew Arnold's) if they
contain life.

Every reader, every writer, is to some extent a prisoner of
time. In our time, for example, advances in space technology
have made the physical location of heavenly mansions difficult
to believe in. But we can exaggerate the literal-mindedness of
the past; they used a convention of symbols for the imageless –
angels with harps, God with a white beard – still beloved of
newspaper cartoonists. Perhaps it is we who are literal-minded.
Not long ago a leading churchman guilelessly claimed that his
doubts about the Ascension of Christ were remedied by his own
experience of going up in a hot-air balloon. (Where there is the
human, the comic is never far away.) As for what might have
been generally thought divine interventions, accesses of grace,
inspirations, we now know just enough about the chemistries of
the body, about psychology, about the unconscious tyrannies
of nature and nurture, to treat these with caution. Also, a faith
in the perfectibility of any political system, once a powerful
source of hope, and therefore of consolation, has suffered severe
blows.

Consolation, therefore, of the traditional kind, is hard to
come by in contemporary literature. Where it exists in the
personal life of a writer it is usually kept private. No one wants
to be thought credulous. A novelist admitted recently that she
had never managed to put what she really believed into her

books, because 'it always sounded so silly'. She was a practising Christian, but found it difficult to admit even that in the interview, in so many words, precisely because to say it properly would take so many words. It is not a question of misleading, or of not coming clean; it can be a properly intellectual diffidence, a recognition of how stale the language of that sort of affirmation has become.

Any compilation such as this must be among other things a history of the use of language, of how people have faced their situation and put it into words; and, as has been said, the words of previous generations can jar. In his book of essays, *Haydn and the Valve Trumpet*, Craig Raine gives an interesting example: he quotes T. S. Eliot, who is engaged in his long argument with Matthew Arnold's idea that poetry is fundamentally 'uplifting'. Eliot asks, 'Can we say that Shakespeare's poetry is great because of the extraordinary power with which Shakespeare feels estimable feelings?' He expects our answer to be 'no', but the odd word there is 'feels'. We seldom ask what Shakespeare, the great ventriloquist, 'feels'. He certainly sometimes expresses the 'estimable', and if you replace 'feels' by 'expresses', you have a less loaded question. But in answer to what Eliot actually asks, Raine says, 'the question answers itself. We don't go to Shakespeare for uplift.' Many might respond – certainly Arnold, probably Leopardi, though he would flinch at the crudity of the formulation – that is precisely why they do go to Shakespeare: to see good, evil, the mixture, the complexity and contradiction, brilliantly paraded; and leave 'uplifted', or 'animated' or 'rekindled' by the knowledge that a fellow-human, not a god, has seen (and felt), god-like, so much that we recognize to be true. Raine would not deny this; the trouble is in the word 'uplift', which would have been acceptable two generations ago, but since then has been in the wrong sort of mouth, has taken on poisonous cargo, become polluted.

Even the word 'consolation' is slippery, for there is none, in the sense that we all lose, being mortal. Perhaps it can only be properly used as it is in 'consolation prize', something awarded to a loser, but one who has done well. Or we can try to define it by deciding what it is not. It is not 'solace', which is shorter-term, and it is greater than 'distraction', which is by definition superficial. One odd thing about consolation is that we do not always know when we receive it, or not straight away. It is sometimes no more than a hint. Writers (or anyone – perhaps it is more likely to be anyone, but here we are dealing with consolations that have been written down) can sometimes let fall something that lies at the bottom of our minds, and rises to the surface when we need it. When Gerard Manley Hopkins says, 'My own heart let me more have pity on,' the unusual word-order may make it memorable, but the idea is of little use when we are on good terms with ourselves, possibly helpful when we are in a mood of self-blame. Likewise, if we are bored on some social occasion and ask ourselves why we bothered to come, Boswell's question to Johnson, why do we gather together socially, when the talk is often so silly, and Johnson's reply, 'to promote kindness', is like the unlocking of a door.

Should we ask what we need consolation for, 'mortality' is too quick an answer. We think of that as little as we can – the dying Brendan Behan said he'd rather be dead than think about death – more often it is the dailyness of unsatisfactory experience that we need to be fortified against. Shakespeare made a useful list: 'And art made tongue-tied by authority, And folly, doctor-like, controlling skill, And simple truth miscalled simplicity, And captive good attending captain ill . . .' For three thousand years, or as far as written records survive, we have been trying to formulate a proper attitude to these ills, as well as to our own mortality, trying to construct a rational and spiritual base for decent living, one not undermined by wishful-thinking, or complacence – those two moles tunnelling and undermining all but the most stoutly constructed systems.

At times we are forced to think about death by a personal grief. But then we are usually made incapable of reading at all, because everything seems either piffling or irrelevant. Here a personal reminiscence might be a clue to some of the selections here. When in such a condition myself (and each case is different) the first book it became possible to read was the prose *Autobiographies* of W. B. Yeats. This was surprising, for certainly they were not relevant. The reason, arrived at long after, must be that they are by a man who took a fundamentally imaginative, and liberally religious, view of life, and saw it – his own life and those of his friends and enemies – as being of heroic, you could say of epic, size. He does this without unacceptable boasting, and his effect is to produce a view of life large enough for any private emotion to be included. Therefore, it consoled. (He even manages to make his poor, hypochondriac uncle seem bright as a figure in a tapestry; all he describes is as though interwoven with golden thread.) Thornton Wilder makes his Julius Caesar say, as he sits by the dying Catullus, that we should always praise life to those who are leaving it. That sounds a paradox, but is an insight (one denied to William Hazlitt, as we shall see), because in ultimate situations – 'At last, the distinguished thing,' said the dying Henry James – it is grandeur we need to be assured of; we know the pettiness.

However, that example of Yeats's prose found unexpectedly consoling is an indication of a danger, of how personal any selection of consolations must inevitably be. It would be easy to go off at tangents – consolation in P. G. Wodehouse, in descriptions of meals, and so on. To avoid too much idio-syncrasy of that kind, the emphasis here is on people who address the subject directly, attempt specifically to console themselves and others. But even this, however profound, would be too monotone on its own. The mood has to be changed constantly if it is to be true to life; and because there are other ways by which consolation can be transmitted. By fellow-feeling, for example: when Montaigne talks at length, and chirpily, about his appalling memory, his account is not only funny, it can console those who suffer similarly, and even those with good memories can be fortified by the cheerfulness and honesty of his self-description.

There could be something dubious about the very idea of consolation, post-Darwin, Marx, Freud, the death camps; our idea of ourselves has changed. Some might feel, stoically, that we must do without it altogether, and shut up; but the Stoics themselves had a great deal to say on the matter. Besides, there can be a grisly sort of satisfaction in the refusal to be consoled, like the Saul Bellow character in *Herzog*, who believed that 'truth is only true as it brings down more disgrace and dreari-ness on human beings, so that if it shows anything but evil it is an illusion, and not truth'. Bellow appears to think this is a modern disease, and it is in the air, but Sydney Smith has some firm words to say on the subject, and Thomas Love Peacock continually mocks it.

For those who have doubts about consolation, it is surely true that most of us who read have had the experience of picking up a book and, possibly unexpectedly, perhaps all the better if so, finding something that briefly restores a faith in our human capacity for goodness, or shores up some part of our sagging courage. At the least, we can recognize the reaction of the severely melancholic William Cowper, when he came across the poems of George Herbert: 'though I found not here what I might have found – a cure for my malady, yet it never seemed so much alleviated as while I was reading him'.

As has been said, not everything here is at first sight 'cheering'; such a collection would end up by depressing us. But, as Francis Bacon says, 'even in the Old Testament, if you listen to David's harp, you shall hear as many hearse-like airs as carols: and the pencil of the Holy Ghost hath laboured more in describing the afflictions of Job than the felicities of Solomon'. (There is consolation in good writing; the cadence of Bacon's phrases, the notion of the Holy Ghost's pencil.)

Francis Bacon was writing a long time ago. Whether we find interest, even help, in the varieties of consolations sought by people in the past depends on whether we believe in the continuity and similarity of human experience. When we see that Seneca, for example, is engaged with the same problems as, say, Simone Weil, we can feel a consoling sense of continuity. Perhaps that is a second, though connected, motive for putting this collection together. We seem to be losing our sense of the past. When someone on the radio says, in 1991, 'but that was back in 1987 . . .', there is sometimes an incredulous note, as though the reference is to an age already difficult to understand, when people were thinking differently, as well as wearing trousers of a different width. This leaves us at the mercy of fashion, where some would like to keep us. Its result is a starvation of the imagination, an inability to connect. Therefore a reminder of past voices, with more recent ones mixed in, collected together and addressing the same subject, is not dissimilar in educative intention from those little boxes of 'Great Works', in uniform bindings, which did so much to spread, and therefore democratize, literacy among the Victorians; 'Great Works' are much too important and useful to be left to specialists.

Certain voices recur; it has been difficult to stop some of them from taking over the conversation. Walt Whitman is a talking-head that kept bobbing up, and as fast as it was pushed down it emerged again, still talking on the matter in hand, because, after all, he wrote a whole book with nothing but consolation for its subject. Sometimes the quotations develop into a conversation, nearly a row, and strong personalities need a chairman, or at least an invisible host. So these evidences, reports, howls, songs, shouts, jokes, have been forced, with some violence, into groups. Violence, because they sometimes continue shouting at each other when separated, and clamour, sometimes, that they find themselves in the wrong company. Nevertheless, readers have to know roughly where they are, or risk being overwhelmed, so the groupings have been given titles.

Christianity, in the strict sense of Incarnation and Redemption, is, or can be, a source of consolation for those who believe in it; not so for those who do not, even though they can still enjoy the visions and poems it has given rise to. Therefore, as far as possible, Christianity-derived consolation has been given a place of its own. But *Personal Faith* (involving some kind of transcendental belief) could not be kept entirely separate from it, as Christianity has flavoured most European writing for fifteen hundred years. An attempt is made, in all the sections, to help each piece of writing flow reasonably smoothly into the next, without too startling a change of tone or direction. Many of the voices refuse to keep to the tone or point required of them – after all, they cannot hear each other, or the chairman, and would probably take no notice of each other or him if they could – so further small introductions are given at the beginning of each section, with a brief explanation of why some of the pieces are there, in case it might not be obvious.

Oddly enough, what has been most consoling, uplifting, animating, in this task (what has done most to kindle enthusiasm) is the evidence of an unfailing fascination with ourselves. Schopenhauer, that doughty, persecuted non-believer – also respectfully intelligent about Christianity – puts it wittily in his *Notebook*, so that it is impossible not to laugh. (The italics are his.)

If everyone did not take such an excessive and exaggerated *interest in himself*, life would be so uninteresting that no one would put up with it.

LOVE

Love, human love, makes an obvious beginning – the first of consolations – and love in the Garden of Eden. It is a consolation in itself that we can even imagine a paradise on earth, and a consolation that we can describe it as well as Milton does.

Charlotte Brontë can also imagine an Adam and Eve-like union of the sexes, and at the back of our minds is always the question: if we can imagine it, why should it not be attainable?

John Clare is also thinking along the clear lines of Charlotte Brontë, in his own way. Keats, ill, in love, is disjointed, defiant, hopeful, fearful.

Human love as a means of transcendence, married love as a conqueror of time. Suckling making as light as he can of the matter. Lovers can separate for all sorts of reasons, but it is sure they will be separated in the end; Simone Weil draws her conclusion, which is, as is usual with her, both practical and transcendental.

1	2	3	4	5	6	7	8	9	10	11	12	13	14	15	16	17	18	19	20
21	22	23	24	25	26	27	28	29	30	31	32	33	34	35	36	37	38	39	40
41	42	43	44	45	46	47	48	49	50	51	52	53	54	55	56	57	58	59	60
61	62	63	64	65	66	67	68	69	70	71	72	73	74	75	76	77	78	79	80
81	82	83	84	85	86	87	88	89	90	91	92	93	94	95	96	97	98	99	100
101	102	103	104	105	106	107	108	109	110	111	112	113	114	115	116	117	118	119	120
121	122	123	124	125	126	127	128	129	130	131	132	133	134	135	136	137	138	139	140
141	142	143	144	145	146	147	148	149	150	151	152	153	154	155	156	157	158	159	160
161	162	163	164	165	166	167	168	169	170	171	172	173	174	175	176	177	178	179	180
181	182	183	184	185	186	187	188	189	190	191	192	193	194	195	196	197	198	199	200
201	202	203	204	205	206	207	208	209	210	211	212	213	214	215	216	217	218	219	220

So hand in hand they passed, the loveliest pair
That ever since in love's embraces met,
Adam the goodliest man of men since born
His sons, the fairest of her daughters Eve.
Under a tuft of shade that on a green
Stood whispering soft, by a fresh fountain side
They sat them down, and after no more toil
Of their sweet gardening labour than sufficed
To recommend cool zephyr, and made ease
More easy, wholesome thirst and appetite
More grateful, to their supper fruits they fell,
Nectarine fruits which the compliant boughs
Yielded them, sidelong as they sat recline
On the soft downy bank damasked with flowers:
The savoury pulp they chew, and in the rind
Still as they thirsted scoop the brimming stream;
Nor gentle purpose, nor endearing smiles
Wanted, nor youthful dalliance as beseems
Fair couple, linked in happy nuptial league,
Alone as they. About them frisking played
All beasts of the earth, since wild, and of all chase
In wood or wilderness, forest or den;
Sporting the lion ramped, and in his paw
Dandled the kid; bears, tigers, ounces, pards,
Gambolled before them, the unwieldly elephant
To make them mirth used all his might, and wreathed
His lithe proboscis; close the serpent sly
Insinuating, wove with Gordian twine
His braided train, and of his fatal guile
Gave proof unheeded; others on the grass
Couched, and now filled with pasture gazing sat,
Or bedward ruminating: for the sun

Declined was hasting now with prone career
To the Ocean Isles, and in the ascending scale
Of heaven the stars that usher evening rose.

JOHN MILTON (1608–74), *Paradise Lost*

I have now been married ten years. I know what it is to live entirely for and with what I love best on earth. I hold myself supremely blest – blest beyond what language can express, because I am my husband's life as fully as he is mine. No woman was ever nearer to her mate than I am – ever more absolutely bone of his bone, and flesh of his flesh. I know no weariness of my Edward's society – he knows none of mine, any more than we each do of the pulsation of the heart that beats in our separate bosoms; consequently, we are ever together. To be together is for us to be at once as free as in solitude, as gay as in company. We talk, I believe, all day long: to talk to each other is but a more animated and an audible thinking. All my confidence is bestowed on him, all his confidence is devoted to me; we are precisely suited in character – perfect concord is the result.

CHARLOTTE BRONTË (1816–55), *Jane Eyre*

My dearest Girl,

Indeed I will not deceive you with respect to my health. This is the fact as far as I know. I have been confined three weeks and am not yet well – this proves that there is something wrong about me which my constitution will either conquer or give way to. Let us hope for the best. Do you hear the thrush singing over the field? I think it is a sign of mild weather – so much the better for me. Like all sinners now I am ill I philosophise aye out of my attachment to every thing, trees, flowers, thrushes, spring, summer, claret &c &c – aye every thing but you – my sister would be glad of my company a little longer. That Thrush is a fine fellow I hope he was fortunate in his choice this year. Do not send any more of my books home. I have a great pleasure in the thought of you looking on them.

Ever yours, my sweet Fanny

J. K.

JOHN KEATS (1795–1821), letter to Fanny Brawne

Soft falls the sweet evening
   Bright shines the one star
The night clouds they're leaning
   On mountains afar
The moon in dim brightness
   The fern in its lightness
Tinge the valley with whiteness
   Both near and afar

O soft falls the evening
   Around those sweet glens
The hill's shadows leaning
   Half over the glen
There meet me my deary
   I'm lonely and weary
And nothing can cheer me
   So meet me agen

The gate it clap'd slightly
   The noise it was small
The footstep fell lightly
   And she pass'd the stone wall
And is it my deary
   I'm no longer weary
But happy and cheery
   For in thee I meet all

JOHN CLARE (1793–1864), 'Song'

When in any way she appeared, just through the hope of receiving her marvellous greeting, I had no enemies left but was instead possessed by such a flame of charity that I was made to forgive all those who had injured me; and if at that moment someone had asked me a question about any matter in the world, my answer, with my face clothed in humility, would have been quite simply: 'Love'.

DANTE (1265–1321), La Vita Nuova

All kings, and all their favourites,
All glory of honours, beauties, wits,
The sun itself, which makes times, as they pass,
Is elder by a year now, than it was
When thou and I first one another saw:
All other things to their destruction draw,
Only our love hath no decay;
This, no tomorrow hath, nor yesterday,
Running it never runs from us away,
But truly keeps his first, last, everlasting day.

Two graves must hide thine and my corse,
If one might, death were no divorce.
Alas, as well as other princes, we
(Who prince enough in one another be)
Must leave at last in death, these eyes, and ears,
Oft fed with true oaths, and with sweet salt tears;
But souls where nothing dwells but love
(All other thoughts being inmates) then shall prove
This, or a love increased there above,
When bodies to their graves, souls from their graves remove.

And then we shall be throughly blessed,
But we no more than all the rest.
Here upon earth, we are kings, and none but we
Can be such kings, nor of such subjects be;
Who is so safe as we? where none can do
Treason to us, except one of us two.
True and false fears let us refrain,
Let us love nobly, and live, and add again
Years and years unto years, till we attain
To write threescore: this is the second of our reign.

JOHN DONNE (1572–1631), 'The Anniversary'

Let me not to the marriage of true minds
   Admit impediments: love is not love
Which alters when it alteration finds,
   Or bends with the remover to remove.
O no, it is an ever-fixèd mark
   That looks on tempests and is never shaken;
It is the star to every wandering bark,
   Whose worth's unknown, although his height be taken.
Love's not Time's fool, though rosy lips and cheeks
   Within his bending sickle's compass come;
Love alters not with his brief hours and weeks,
   But bears it out even to the edge of doom.
     If this be error, and upon me proved,
     I never writ, nor no man ever loved.

         WILLIAM SHAKESPEARE (1564–1616)

   Twenty years hence my eyes may grow
   If not quite dim, yet rather so,
   Still yours from others they shall know
          Twenty years hence.
   Twenty years hence, tho' it may hap
   That I be called to take a nap
   In a cool cell where thunder-clap
          Was never heard,
   There breathe but o'er my arch of grass
   A not too sadly sighed *Alas*,
   And I shall catch, ere you can pass,
          That wingéd word.

      WALTER SAVAGE LANDOR (1775–1864)

   John Anderson my jo, John,
     When we were first acquent,
   Your locks were like the raven,
     Your bonny brow was brent;
   But now your brow is bald, John,
     Your locks are like the snow,
   But blessings on your frosty pow
     John Anderson, my jo.

John Anderson my jo, John,
  We clamb the hill together,
And many a canty day, John,
  We've had wi' one another;
Now we maun totter down, John,
  And hand in hand we'll go,
And sleep together at the foot,
  John Anderson, my jo.

ROBERT BURNS (1759–96)

Sigh no more Ladies, sigh no more,
  Men were deceivers ever;
One foot in sea, and one on shore,
  To one thing constant never.
Then sigh not so, but let them go,
  And be you blithe and bonny,
Converting all your sounds of woe
  Into hey nonny nonny.

Sing no more ditties, sing no moe
  Of dumps so dull and heavy;
The fraud of men were ever so
  Since summer first was leavy.
Then sigh not so, but let them go,
  And be you blithe and bonny,
Converting all your sounds of woe
  Into hey nonny nonny.

WILLIAM SHAKESPEARE, *Much Ado About Nothing*

Why so pale and wan, fond lover?
    Prithee, why so pale?
Will, when looking well can't move her,
    Looking ill prevail?
    Prithee, why so pale?

Why so dull and mute, young sinner?
    Prithee, why so mute?

Will, when speaking well can't win her,
    Saying nothing do 't?
    Prithee, why so mute?

Quit, quit for shame, this will not move,
    This cannot take her;
If of herself she will not love,
    Nothing can make her:
    The devil take her.

                  SIR JOHN SUCKLING (1609–41)

Sometimes with one I love I fill myself with rage for fear I
    effuse unreturned love,
But now I think there is no unreturned love, the pay is
    certain one way or another,
(I loved a certain person ardently and my love was not
    returned.
Yet out of that I have written these songs.)

                WALT WHITMAN (1819–92), *Leaves of Grass*

Most glorious Lord of life, that on this day
    didst make thy triumph over death and sin,
    and having harrowed hell, didst bring away
    captivity thence captive us to win;
This joyous day, dear Lord, with joy begin,
    and grant that we for whom thou diddest die
    being with thy dear blood clean washed from sin,
    may live for ever in felicity.
And that thy love we weighing worthily,
    may likewise love thee for the same again,
    and for thy sake that all like dear didst buy,
    with love may one another entertain.
So let us love, dear love, like as we ought;
    love is the lesson which the Lord us taught.

                EDMUND SPENSER (1552–99)

And then one or other dies. And we think of this as love cut short; like a dance stopped in mid career or a flower with its head unluckily snapped off – something truncated and therefore, lacking its due shape. I wonder. If, as I can't help suspecting, the dead also feel the pains of separation (and this may be one of their purgatorial sufferings), then for both lovers, and for all pairs of lovers without exception, bereavement is a universal and integral part of our experience of love. It follows marriage as normally as marriage follows courtship or as autumn follows summer. It is not a truncation of the process but one of its phases; not the interruption of the dance, but the next figure. We are 'taken out of ourselves' by the loved one while she is here. Then comes the tragic figure of the dance in which we must learn to be still taken out of ourselves though the bodily presence is withdrawn, to love the very Her, and not fall back to loving our past, or our memory, or our sorrow, or our relief from sorrow, or our own love.

C. S. LEWIS (1898–1963), A Grief Observed

It is only necessary to know that love is a direction and not a state of the soul. If one is unaware of this, one falls into despair at the first onslaught of affliction.

SIMONE WEIL (1909–43), Waiting on God

CHRISTIANITY

Christianity: doctrinal mostly, or dependent on doctrine, from various angles. G. K. Chesterton is given space to express himself because, although technically not a Christian at the time he wrote these words, he is defining what sounds like the basis of his thought.

After Cowper's 'Light Shining Out of Darkness' there is a series of more particular grapplings with the Christian life.

One departure from orthodox Christianity proved irresistible: Cardinal Newman and W. H. Auden fit into a little triptych with the very heterodox John Cowper Powys, because they make the same affirmation of hope, and for the same reason.

Lastly I give the poor
woman, my mother, who bore
much pain for me – God knows!
this prayer to our Mistress,
Mary, my house and fortress
against the ills and sorrows
of life. I have no other
patron, nor has my mother.

'Lady of heaven, queen of the world,
and ruler of the underworld,
receive your humble Christian child,
and let him live with those you save;
although my soul is not much worth
saving, my Mistress and My Queen,
your grace is greater than my sin –
without you no man may deserve,
or enter heaven. I do not lie:
in this faith let me live and die.

'Say to your Son that I am his;
Mary of Egypt was absolved,
also the clerk, Theophilus,
whom you consented to restore,
although he'd made a pact with hell.
Save me from ever doing such ill,
our bond with evil is dissolved,
Oh Virgin, undefiled, who bore
Christ whom we celebrate at Mass –
in this faith let me live and die.

'I am a woman – poor, absurd,
who never learned to read your word –

at Mass each Sunday, I have seen
a painted paradise with lutes
and harps, a hell that boils the damned:
one gives me joy, the other doubts.
Oh let me have your joy, my Queen,
bountiful, honest and serene,
by whom no sinner is condemned –
in this faith let me live and die.

'You bore, oh Virgin and Princess,
Jesus, whose Kingdom never ends –
Our Lord took on our littleness,
and walked the world to save his friends –
he gave his lovely youth to death,
that's why I say to my last breath
in this faith let me live and die.'

FRANÇOIS VILLON (1431–*c*.63),
version by Robert Lowell,
'Prayer for his mother to say to the Virgin'

What makes me love you O my God, is not
the heaven you have promised me, nor does
the hell I fear so greatly make me stop
the pain I cause you by my sinfulness.

You, my Lord, make me love you: when I see
you hammered to that cross, shamed and defiled,
and see the wounds inflicted on your body,
how they insulted you, and how you died.

And most of all, your love for me. So even if heaven
did not exist, I would love you as much, and even
if hell did not exist, I would fear your anger.

You do not need to reward me in exchange:
as even if I did not have the hope I do
I would love you no less than I love you now.

ANON. (sixteenth-century Spanish), 'To Christ Crucified'

Albion replied: Cannot Man exist without mysterious
Offering of self for another? is this Friendship and
    Brotherhood?
I see thee in the likeness and similitude of Los my friend.

Jesus said: Wouldest thou love one who never died
For thee, or ever die for one who had not died for thee?
And if God dieth not for Man, Man could not exist; for Man
    is love
As God is love: every kindness to another is a little death
In the divine image, nor can man exist except by
    brotherhood.

WILLIAM BLAKE (1757–1827), from *Jerusalem*

Wilt thou forgive that sin where I begun,
    Which is my sin, though it were done before?
Wilt thou forgive those sins through which I run,
    And do them still; though still I do deplore?
        When thou hast done, thou hast not done,
            For, I have more.

Wilt thou forgive that sin by which I won
    Others to sin? and made my sin their door?
Wilt thou forgive that sin which I did shun
    A year, or two; but wallowed in a score?
        When thou hast done, thou hast not done,
            For, I have more.

I have a sin of fear, that when I have spun
    My last thread, I shall perish at the shore;
Swear by thy self, that at my death thy Sun
    Shall shine as it shines now, and heretofore;
        And, having done that, thou hast done:
            I have no more.

JOHN DONNE (1572–1631), 'A Hymn to God the Father'

With what deep murmurs through time's silent stealth
Doth thy transparent, cool and watery wealth
      Here flowing fall,
      And chide, and call,
As if his liquid, loose retínue stayed
Lingering, and were of this steep place afraid,
      The common pass
      Where, clear as glass,
      All must descend
      Not to an end:
But quickened by this deep and rocky grave,
Rise to a longer course more bright and brave.
Dear stream! dear bank, where often I
Have sat, and pleased my pensive eye,
Why, since each drop of thy quick store
Runs thither, whence it flowed before,
Should poor souls fear a shade or night,
Who came (sure) from a sea of light?
Or since those drops are all sent back
So sure to thee, that none doth lack,
Why should frail flesh doubt any more
That what God takes, he'll not restore?
O useful element and clear!
My sacred wash and cleanser here,
My first consigner unto those
Fountains of life, where the Lamb goes?
What sublime truths, and wholesome themes,
Lodge in thy mystical, deep streams!
Such as dull man can never find
Unless that Spirit lead his mind
Which first upon thy face did move,
And hatched all with his quickening love.
As this loud brook's incessant fall
In streaming rings restagnates all
Which reach by course the bank, and then
Are no more seen, just so pass men.
O my invisible estate,
My glorious liberty, still late!
Thou art the channel my soul seeks,
Not this with cataracts and creeks.

HENRY VAUGHAN (1622–95), 'The Waterfall'

If it be granted that this primary devotion to a place or thing is a source of creative energy, we can pass on to a very peculiar fact. Let us reiterate for an instant that the only right optimism is a sort of universal patriotism. What is the matter with the pessimist? I think it can be stated by saying that he is the cosmic anti-patriot. And what is the matter with the anti-patriot? I think it can be stated, without undue bitterness, by saying that he is the candid friend. And what is the matter with the candid friend? There we strike the rock of real life and immutable human nature.

I venture to say that what is bad in the candid friend is simply that he is not candid. He is keeping something back – his own gloomy pleasure in saying unpleasant things . . .

On the other side our idealist pessimists were represented by the old remnant of the Stoics. Marcus Aurelius and his friends had really given up the idea of any god in the universe and looked only to the god within. They had no hope of any virtue in nature, and hardly any hope of any virtue in society. They had not enough interest in the outer world really to wreck or revolutionise it. They did not love the city enough to set fire to it. Thus the ancient world was exactly in our own desolate dilemma. The only people who really enjoyed this world were busy breaking it up; and the virtuous people did not care enough about them to knock them down. In this dilemma (the same as ours) Christianity suddenly stepped in and offered a singular answer, which the world eventually accepted as *the* answer. It was the answer then, and I think it is the answer now.

This answer was like the slash of a sword; it sundered; it did not in any sense sentimentally unite. Briefly, it divided God from the cosmos. That transcendence and distinctness of the deity which some Christians now want to remove from Christianity, was really the only reason why any one wanted to be a Christian. It was the whole point of the Christian answer to the unhappy pessimist and the still more unhappy optimist. As I am here only concerned with their particular problem I shall indicate only briefly this great metaphysical suggestion. All descriptions of the creating or sustaining principle in things must be metaphorical, because they must be verbal. Thus the pantheist is forced to speak of God *in* all things as if he were in a box. Thus the evolutionist has, in his very name, the idea of being unrolled like a carpet. All terms, religious and irreligious, are open to this charge. The only question is whether all terms are useless, or whether one can, with such a phrase, cover a distinct *idea* about the origin of things. I think one can, and so evidently does the evolutionist, or he would not talk about evolution. And the root phrase for all Christian theism was this, that God was a creator, as an artist is a creator. A poet is so separate from his poem that he himself speaks of it as a little thing he has 'thrown off'. Even in giving it forth he has flung it away. This principle that all creation and procreation is a breaking off is at least as consistent through the cosmos as the evolutionary principle that all growth is a branching out. A woman loses a child even in having a child. All creation is separation. Birth is as solemn a parting as death.

It was the prime philosophic principle of Christianity that this divorce in the divine act of making (such as severs the poet from the poem or the mother from the new-born child) was the true description of the act whereby the absolute energy made the world. According to most philosophers, God in making the world enslaved it. According to Christianity, in making it, He set it free. God has written, not so much a poem, but rather a play; a play He had planned as perfect, but which had necessarily been left to human actors and stage-managers, who had since made a great mess of it.

G. K. CHESTERTON (1874–1936), *Orthodoxy*

It was His wisdom made you need the sun. It was His goodness made you need the sea. Be sensible of what you need, or enjoy neither. Consider how much you need them. For thence they derive their value. Suppose the sun were extinguished; or the sea were dry. There would be no light, no beauty, no warmth, no fruits, no flowers, no pleasant gardens, feasts, or prospects. No wine no oil no bread, no life, no motion. Would you not give all the gold and silver in the Indies for such a treasure? Prize it now you have it, at that rate, and you shall be a grateful creature; nay you shall be a divine and heavenly person. For they in heaven do prize blessings when they have them. They in earth when they have them prize them not; they in hell prize them, when they have them not.

THOMAS TRAHERNE (1637–74)

The world is charged with the grandeur of God.
    It will flame out, like shining from shook foil;
    It gathers to a greatness, like the ooze of oil
Crushed. Why do men then now not reck his rod?
Generations have trod, have trod, have trod;
    And all is seared with trade; bleared, smeared with toil;
    And wears man's smudge and shares man's smell: the soil
Is bare now, nor can foot feel, being shod.

And, for all this, nature is never spent;
    There lives the dearest freshness deep down things;
And though the last lights off the black West went
    Oh, morning, at the brown brink eastward, springs –
Because the Holy Ghost over the bent
    World broods with warm breast and with ah! bright
        wings.

GERARD MANLEY HOPKINS (1844–89), 'God's Grandeur'

In this same time our Lord showed me a spiritual sight of His close loving.

I saw that he is to us everything that is good and comfortable for us: he is our clothing that for love wrappeth us, claspeth us, and encloseth us round for tender love, that he may never leave us; being to us all that is good, to my understanding.

Also in this he showed me a little thing, the size of a hazel nut, in the palm of my hand; and it was as round as a ball. I looked upon it with eye of my understanding, and thought: *What may this be?* And it was answered thus: *It is all that is made.* I marvelled how it might last, for methought it might suddenly have fallen to naught for littleness. And I was answered in my understanding: *It lasteth, and ever shall last, for that God loveth it.* And so all hath being by the love of God.

In this little thing I saw three properties: the first is that God made it, the second is that God loveth it, the third, that God keepeth it.

JULIAN OF NORWICH (c.1342–c.1416)

Never think of God but as an infinity of overflowing love, who wills nothing by the creation, but to be the comfort, the blessing, and joy of every life according to its capacity. And let this idea, which is the truth of truths, animate and govern all that you think, or say, or do, either towards God, or man.

WILLIAM LAW (1686–1761), from a letter

Thou canst show thy great strength at all times when thou wilt; and who may withstand the power of thine arm? For the whole world before thee is as a little grain of the balance, yea, as a drop of the morning dew that falleth down upon the earth. But thou hast mercy upon all; for thou canst do all things, and winkest at the sins of men, because they should amend. For thou lovest all the things that are, and abhorrest nothing which thou hast made: for never wouldest thou have made any thing, if thou hadst hated it. And how could any thing have endured, if it had not been thy will? or been preserved, if not called by thee? But thou sparest all: for they are thine, O Lord, thou lover of souls.

The Wisdom of Solomon (1st century BC)

I come at last to what I have called your old perpetual complaint, in which you presume to blame God for the manner of our entry into religion instead of wishing to glorify him as you justly should. I had thought that this bitterness of heart at what was so clear an act of divine mercy had long since disappeared. The more dangerous such bitterness is to you in wearing out body and soul alike, the more pitiful it is and distressing to me. If you are anxious to please me in everything, as you claim, and in this at least would end my torment, or even give me the greatest pleasure, you must rid yourself of it. If it persists you can neither please me nor attain bliss with me. Can you bear me to come to this without you – I whom you declare yourself ready to follow to the very fires of hell? Seek piety in this at least, lest you cut yourself off from me who am hastening, you believe, towards God; be the readier to do so because the goal we must come to will be blessed, and our companionship the more welcome for being happier . . .

See then, my beloved, see how with the dragnets of this mercy the Lord has fished us up from the depth of this dangerous sea, and from the abyss of what a Charybdis he has saved our shipwrecked selves, although we were unwilling, so that each of us may justly break out in that cry: 'The Lord takes thought for me' . . .

Come too, my inseparable companion, and join me in thanksgiving, you who were made my partner both in guilt and in grace.

PETER ABELARD (1079–1142), from a letter to Heloise

'But tell me, you who are living here in bliss,
do you ever wish you were in a higher place,
to see Him more, or to grow closer to Him?'

She and the other shades smiled at each other
a little, and then she answered, with such joy
she seemed to glow with love, with first love's fire.

'O brother, all our wants are satisfied
by virtue of Love, that makes us wish for only
the things we have, and thirst for nothing else.

If we did wish to be higher than we are,
the desires we had would be out of harmony
with the will of Him who chose to set us here;

and this, you will see, can not be, in these spheres,
as Love is the essence of our being here,
and if you remember what Love truly is.

It is the nature of this blessed state
that we should live within the will of God
so that our will and His may be the same;

and His will is our peace. It is the sea
to which all things are flowing: those that are
created by that Will, and formed by nature.'

Then I saw clearly how each part of Heaven
is all of Paradise; even when the grace
of the utmost Good is shed in different ways.

DANTE (1265–1321), *Paradiso*

God moves in a mysterious way
    His wonders to perform;
He plants his footsteps in the sea,
    And rides upon the storm.

Deep in unfathomable mines
    Of never-failing skill,
He treasures up his bright designs,
    And works his sovereign will.

Ye fearful saints, fresh courage take,
    The clouds ye so much dread
Are big with mercy, and shall break
    In blessings on your head.

Judge not the Lord by feeble sense,
    But trust him for his grace;
Behind a frowning providence
    He hides a smiling face.

His purposes will ripen fast,
    Unfolding every hour;
The bud may have a bitter taste,
    But sweet will be the flower.

Blind unbelief is sure to err,
 And scan his work in vain:
God is his own interpreter,
 And He will make it plain.

WILLIAM COWPER (1731–1800),
'Light Shining out of Darkness'

Discipline of the Spirit. 'In a sense Luther took the matter too lightly. He ought to have made it apparent that the freedom he was fighting for led to making life, the spiritual life, infinitely more exhausting than it had been before.'

It is typical of Kierkegaard to put it in this baleful way. Tourville is saying the same kind of things, and much better, in this passage:

> We must follow our own path and not worry about the puddles into which we fall; otherwise we should never move on at all . . . I wish so much that you could get hold of what perfection in this world consists of. It is not like going up a great hill from which we see an ever-widening landscape, a greater horizon, a plain receding further and further into the distance. It is more like an overgrown path which we cannot find; we grope about; we are caught by brambles; we lose all sense of the distance covered; we do not know whether we are going round and round or whether we are advancing. We are certain only of one thing; that we desire to go on however worn and tired we are. That is your life and you should rejoice greatly because of it, for it is a true life, serious and real, on which God opens His eyes and His heart.

Wonderful! A passage to read again and again, and particularly when lost in the brambles.

PHILIP TOYNBEE (1916–81), *End of a Journey*

From being anxious, or secure,
Dead clods of sadness, or light squibs of mirth;
From thinking, that great courts immure
All, or no happiness, or that this earth
Is only for our prison framed;
Or that thou art covetous
To them whom thou lov'st, or that they are maimed
From reaching this world's sweet, who seek thee thus
With all their might: Good Lord deliver us.

From needing danger, to be good;
From owing thee yesterday's tears today;
From trusting so much to thy blood
That in that hope we wound our soul away;
From bribing thee with alms, to excuse
Some sin more burdenous;
From light affecting, in religion, news,
From thinking us all soul, neglecting thus
Our mutual duties: Lord deliver us.

From tempting Satan to tempt us,
By our connivance, or slack company;
From measuring ill by vicious,
Neglecting to choke sin's spawn, vanity;
From indiscreet humility,
Which might be scandalous
And cast reproach on Christianity;
From being spies, or to spies pervious,
From thirst, or scorn, of fame: deliver us.

JOHN DONNE (1572–1631), from 'A Litany'

If his wife or any of his children had been diseased, or troubled, he would say to them, 'We may not look at our pleasure to go to heaven in feather beds, it is not the way. For our Lord himself went thither with great pain, and by many tribulations, which is the path wherein he walked thither, and the servant may not look to be in better case than his Master.' And as he would in this sort persuade them to take their troubles patiently, so would he in like case teach them to withstand the devil and his temptations, valiantly saying, 'Whosoever will mark the devil and his temptations shall find him therein much like to an ape. For as an ape not well looked to will be busy and bold to do shrewd turns, and contrariwise being spied will suddenly leap back and adventure no farther: so the devil, seeing a man idle, slothful, and without resistance ready to receive his temptations, waxeth so hardy that he will not fail still to continue with him until to his purpose he hath brought him: but on the other side, if he see a man with diligence present to prevent and withstand his temptations, he waxeth so weary, that in conclusion he forsaketh him. For as much as the devil by disposition is a spirit of nature so envious, that he feareth any more to assault him, lest that he should thereby not only catch a foul fall himself, but also minister to the man more matter of merit.' Thus delighted he evermore not only in virtuous exercises to be occupied himself, but also to exhort his wife, and children, and household, to embrace and follow the same.

WILLIAM ROPER (1498–1578), *Life of Sir Thomas More*

After this the Lord brought to my mind the longing that I had to Him before. And I saw that nothing hindered me but sin. And so I looked upon us all in general, and thought: *If sin had not been, we should all have been clean and like to our Lord, as he made us.* And thus, in my folly, before this time often I wondered why by the great foreseeing wisdom of God the beginning of sin was not prevented: for then, I thought, all should have been well.

This stirring of mind was much to be forsaken, but nevertheless I made mourning and sorrow for it, without reason and discretion. But Jesus, who in this vision informed me of all that is needful to me, answered by this word and said: *Sin is needful; but all shall be well, and all shall be well, and all manner of thing shall be well.*

In this naked word *sin*, our Lord brought to my mind, in general, *all that is not good*; and the shameful scorn and utter desolation that he bore for us in this life, and his dying; and all the pains and passions of all his creatures, ghostly and bodily . . . and the beholding of this, with all pains that ever were or ever shall be – and of all these I understand the passion of Christ as the most pain, above all others. All this was shown in a touch and quickly passed over into comfort, for our good Lord would not that the soul were affeared of this terrible sight . . .

And for the tender love that our good Lord hath to all that shall be saved, he comforteth readily and sweetly, signifying thus: *It is true that sin is cause of all this pain; but all shall be well, and all shall be well, and all manner of thing shall be well.*

These words were said full tenderly, showing no manner of blame to me nor to any that shall be saved. So it would be greatly unnatural to blame or wonder at God for my sin, since he blameth not me for sin. And in these words I saw a marvellous high mystery hid in God, which mystery he shall openly make known to us in Heaven; in which knowing we shall verily see the cause why he suffered sin to come. In which sight we shall endlessly joy in our Lord God.

JULIAN OF NORWICH (*c.*1342–*c.*1416)

Ah my dear angry Lord,
Since thou dost love, yet strike;
Cast down, yet help afford;
Sure I will do the like.

I will complain, yet praise;
I will bewail, approve;
And all my sour-sweet days
I will lament, and love.

GEORGE HERBERT (1593–1633), 'Bitter-sweet'

The Stoics say: 'Retire within yourselves. It is there you will find your rest.' And that is not true.
The others say: 'Go outside; seek happiness in amusements.' And that is not true. Illnesses come.
Happiness is neither without nor within us; it is in God, and both outside and within us.

PASCAL (1623–62), *Pensées*

How much can God work through those who don't believe in him?

This is a hard question indeed. For if, in conscious humility, we say, As easily as he can work through us, then what on earth is the point of all our efforts to make ourselves penetrable; receptive; willing containers for the Spirit? But if we say that God can work only through those who believe in him then how do we explain the extraordinary goodness of so many non-believers? A goodness which goes far beyond what their own rational standards of virtue demand of them.

Things become clearer when we think of the saints; for there have been no rationalist saints; indeed the phrase is self-contradictory, since the saint is a holy man even more essentially than he is a good man. It is even possible to imagine a very good rationalist who is demonstrably more virtuous than a very holy saint. The saint, though consumed by love of God and man, might have sudden lapses – e.g. fits of violent ill-temper – which he would bitterly repent. The good rationalist might be serenely, even ardently benevolent, and never fall from his own high standard. Or if he did fall he would not repent: he would make a sensible resolution not to fall again. There is a great gulf fixed between the two; and how well I understand those who prefer the good, sensible, unpretentious rationalist to the ex-travagant, often wild, often sickly, often 'impossible' figure of the holy man.

Yet it is St Francis who constantly excites my imagination, not John Stuart Mill; and I would rather read a life of General Booth than one of Voltaire.

PHILIP TOYNBEE, *Part of a Journey*

'Pluck up thy courage, faint heart; what though thou be fearful, sorry and weary, and standeth in great dread of most painful torments, be of good comfort; for I myself have vanquished the whole world, and yet felt I far more fear, sorrow, weariness, and much more inward anguish too, when I considered my most bitter, painful Passion to press so fast upon me. He that is strong-hearted may find a thousand glorious valiant martyrs whose example he may right joyously follow. But thou now, O

timorous and weak, silly sheep, think it sufficient for thee only
to walk after me, which am thy shepherd and governor, and so
mistrust thyself and put thy trust in me. Take hold on the hem
of my garment, therefore; from thence shalt thou perceive such
strength and relief to proceed . . .'

SIR THOMAS MORE (?1477–1535), Treatise on the Passion

Dear heart: First I must tell you that quite evidently the last
twenty-four hours of one's life are no different from any others.
I had always imagined that it would come as a shock to say to
oneself: 'Now the sun is setting for the last time for you, now the
hour hand will make only two more revolutions before twelve,
now you are going to bed for the last time.' Nothing of the sort.
Perhaps I am a little cracked. For I cannot deny that I am in
really high spirits. I only pray to God in heaven to sustain me in
this mood, for surely it is easier for the flesh to die in this state.
How merciful the Lord has been to me! Even at the risk of
sounding hysterical – I am so full of thanks that there is actually
no room for anything else. He has guided me so firmly and
clearly during these two days. The whole courtroom might
have roared, like Herr Freisler himself, and all the walls might
have rocked – it would have made no difference to me. It was
just as is written in Isaiah 43:2: 'When thou passest through the
water, I will be with thee; and through the rivers, they shall not
overflow thee: when thou walkest through the fire, thou shalt
not be burned; neither shall the flame kindle upon thee.' That is
to say, upon your soul. When I was called up for my last words,
I was in such a frame of mind that I nearly said, 'I have only one
thing to add to my defence. Take my goods, my honour, my
child and wife; the body they may kill; God's truth abideth still,
his kingdom is for ever.' But that would only have made it
harder for the others, therefore I said only, 'I do not intend to
say anything, Herr President.' . . .

Therefore I can say only one thing, dear heart. May God be
as merciful to you as to me – then even the death of a husband
matters not at all. For he can demonstrate his omnipotence
even when you are making pancakes for the boys, or when you
have to take Puschti out of the room (although I hope that isn't

necessary any more). I should be saying farewell to you – I can't do it. I should be mourning and regretting the drabness of your everyday life – I can't do it. I should indeed be thinking of the burdens that will now fall upon you – I can't do it. I can say only one thing to you: if you attain to a feeling of supreme security – if the Lord gives you that which, had it not been for this period in our lives and its conclusion, you would never have had, then I am leaving you a treasure that cannot be confiscated, a treasure compared to which even my life is of small account . . .

The decisive pronouncement in my trial was: 'Count Moltke, Christianity and we National Socialists have one thing in common, and one thing only: we claim the whole man.' Did he realize what he was saying? Just think how wondrously God prepared this unworthy vessel of his: at the very moment when there was danger of my being drawn into active preparations for the coup I was taken out of it, so that I am free and remain free of any connection with the use of violence. In addition, God had implanted in me that socialistic trait which freed me, although owner of a great estate, from any suspicion of representing vested interests. Then he abased me as I have never been abased before, so that I have had to give over all pride, so that after thirty-eight years I finally understand my sinfulness, so that I am learning to pray for his forgiveness, to entrust myself to his mercy. Then he caused me to come here, that I might see you standing fast, and that I might be freed of all thoughts of you and the boys, that is to say, all anxious thoughts. He is giving me time and opportunity to put in order everything that can be put in order, so that all earthly cares can fall away. Then he permitted me to experience, to an unheard-of depth, the anguish of parting and the fear of death and the terror of hell – so that this too is over and done with.

Then he endowed me with faith, hope, and love, all this in a plenitude truly lavish . . . And then your husband was selected to be attacked and condemned, as a Protestant, above all because of his friendship with Catholics. And thus he stood before Freisler not as a Protestant, not as a landed proprietor, not as a nobleman, not as a Prussian, not as a German – all that was explicitly eliminated in the main hearing (for example, Sperr said: 'I thought, what an extraordinary Prussian') – but as a Christian and as nothing else . . .

COUNT VON MOLTKE (1907–45), from a letter to his wife

Even such is Time, which takes in trust
Our youth, our joys, and all we have,
And pays us but with age and dust;
Who in the dark and silent grave,
When we have wandered all our ways,
Shuts up the story of our days.
But from which earth and grave and dust
The Lord shall raise me up, I trust.

SIR WALTER RALEGH (?1554–1618)

What, then, is time? I know well enough what it is, provided that nobody asks me; but if I am asked what it is and try to explain, I am baffled. All the same I can confidently say that I know that if nothing passed, there would be no past time; if nothing were going to happen, there would be no future time; and if nothing *were*, there would be no present time.

Of these three divisions of time, then, how can two, the past and the future, *be*, when the past no longer is and the future is not yet? As for the present, if it were always present and never moved on to become the past, it would not be time but eternity. If, therefore, the present is time only by reason of the fact that it moves on to become the past, how can we say that even the present *is*, when the reason why it *is* is that it is *not to be*? In other words, we cannot rightly say that time *is*, except by reason of its impending state of *not being* . . .

You, my Father, are eternal. But I am divided between time gone by and time to come, and its course is a mystery to me. My thoughts, the intimate life of my soul, are torn this way and that in the havoc of change. And so it will be until I am purified and melted by the fire of your love and fused into one with you . . .

Then I shall be cast and set firm in the mould of your truth. I shall no longer suffer the questions of men who, for their punishment, are sick of a disease which makes them thirst for more than they can drink, so that they ask 'What was God doing before he made heaven and earth?' or 'How did it occur to God to create something, when he had never created anything before?'

Grant them, O Lord, to think well what they say and to recognize that 'never' has no meaning when there is no time. If a man is said never to have made anything, it can only mean that he made nothing at any time. Let them see, then, that there cannot possibly be time without creation. Let them have done with this nonsense. Let them instead *be intent on what lies before them.*

ST AUGUSTINE OF HIPPO (354–430), Confessions

When I consider how my light is spent,
Ere half my days, in this dark world and wide,
And that one talent which is death to hide
Lodged with me useless, though my soul more bent
To serve therewith my maker, and present
My true account, lest he returning chide,
Doth God exact day-labour, light denied,
I fondly ask; but Patience to prevent
That murmur, soon replies, God doth not need
Either man's work or his own gifts; who best
Bear his mild yoke, they serve him best; his state
Is kingly. Thousands at his bidding speed
And post o'er land and ocean without rest:
They also serve who only stand and wait.

JOHN MILTON (1608–74), 'On His Blindness'

Having been tenant long to a rich Lord,
  Not thriving, I resolvéd to be bold
And make a suit unto him, to afford
  A new small-rented lease, and cancel the old.
In heaven at his manor I him sought;
  They told me there, that he was lately gone
About some land, which he had dearly bought
  Long since on earth, to take possession.
I straight returned, and knowing his great birth,
  Sought him accordingly in great resorts,
  In cities, theatres, gardens, parks, and courts;
At length I heard a ragged noise and mirth
  Of thieves and murderers: there I him espied,
  Who straight, *Your suit is granted* said, and died.

GEORGE HERBERT (1593–1633), 'Redemption'

Of course the sinner must repent. But why? Simply because
otherwise he would be unable to realise what he had done. The
moment of repentance is the moment of initiation. More than
that. It is the means by which one alters one's past. The Greeks
thought that impossible. They often say in their gnomic apho-
risms 'Even the Gods cannot alter the past.' Christ showed that
the commonest sinner could do it. That it was the one thing he
could do. Christ, had he been asked, would have said – I feel
quite certain about it – that the moment the prodigal son fell on
his knees and wept he really made his having wasted his
substance with harlots, and then kept swine and hungered for
the husks they ate, beautiful and holy incidents in his life. It is
difficult for most people to grasp the idea. I dare say one has to
go to prison to understand it. If so, it may be worth while going
to prison.

OSCAR WILDE (1854–1900), *De Profundis*

If a good man were ever housed in Hell
  By needful error of the qualities,
Perhaps to prove the rule or shame the devil,
  Or speak the truth only a stranger sees,

Would he, surrendering quick to obvious hate,
  Fill half eternity with cries and tears,
Or watch beside Hell's little wicket gate
  In patience for the first ten thousand years,

Feeling the curse climb slowly to his throat
  That, uttered, dooms him to rescindless ill,
Forcing his praying tongue to run by rote,
  Eternity entire before him still?

Would he at last, grown faithful in his station,
  Kindle a little hope in hopeless Hell,
And sow among the damned doubts of damnation,
  Since here someone could live and could live well?

One doubt of evil would bring down such a grace,
  Open such a gate, all Eden could enter in,
Hell be a place like any other place,
  And love and hate and life and death begin.

EDWIN MUIR (1887–1959)

Hope consists in the knowledge that the evil one carries about in oneself is finite, and that the slightest orientation of the soul toward Good, were it to last only an instant, does away with a little of it; and that in the spiritual domain every particle of Good infallibly produces Good.

  This knowledge is experimental, which is why Hope is a supernatural virtue. It represents fearlessness in affairs of the Spirit.

SIMONE WEIL (1909–43), *Notebooks*

As an example of the difficulty of separating observation from interpretation of experience, let me take a trivial personal one. Many people have given accounts of what they experienced while having a tooth extracted under nitrous oxide, and these show close similarities. Thus William James says:

The keynote of it is invariably a reconciliation. It is as if the opposites of the world, whose contradictions and conflict make all our difficulties and troubles, were melted into unity.

My experience, like his, was of two opposites, love in the sense of agape, and hate, but in my case they did not melt into a unity. I felt an absolute conviction about two things: (a) that, ultimately the power of love was greater than the force of hate; (b) that, on the other hand, however great any human being might estimate the force of hate to be, he would always underestimate it. The actual quantity of hate in the universe was greater than any human imagination could conceive. Nevertheless, the power of love was still greater. Would I, I ask myself, have had precisely *this* experience if I had not been brought up in a Christian home and therefore been a person to whom the Christian notion of agape was a familiar one, and I find myself unable to say yes or no with any certainty.

W. H. AUDEN (1907–73), The Protestant Mystics

Starting then with the being of a God (which, as I have said, is as certain to me as the certainty of my own existence, though when I try to put the grounds of that certainty into logical shape I find a difficulty in doing so in mood and figure to my satisfaction), I look out of myself into the world of men, and there I see a sight which fills me with unspeakable distress. The world seems simply to give the lie to that great truth, of which my whole being is so full; and the effect upon me is in consequence, as a matter of necessity, as confusing as if it denied that I am in existence myself. If I looked into a mirror, and did not see my face, I should have the sort of feeling which actually comes upon me, when I look into the living busy world, and see no reflection of its Creator. This is, to me, one of the great difficulties of this absolute primary truth, to which I referred just now. Were it not for this voice, speaking so clearly in my conscience and my heart, I should be an atheist, or a pantheist, or a polytheist, when I looked into the world.

JOHN HENRY NEWMAN (1801–90), Apologia pro Vita Sua

My father was an inarticulate man. I am an only too voluble one. My father was a man of rock. I am a worshipper of the wind. But now when from this resting-place, this ledge, this slab of stone, in the wavering Indian trail of my migrations and reversions, I look back at the path behind me and the path before me it seems as if it had taken me half a century merely to learn with what weapons, and with what surrender of weapons, *I am to begin to live my life.*

The astronomical world is *not* all there is. We are in touch with other dimensions, other levels of life. And from among the powers that spring from these *other levels* there rises up one Power, all the more terrible because it refuses to practise cruelty, a Power that is neither Capitalist, nor Communist, nor Fascist, nor Democratic, nor Nazi, a Power *not of this world at all*, but capable of inspiring the individual soul with the wisdom of the serpent and the harmlessness of the dove.

And thus it comes to pass, even while we are still in life, that when our soul loses itself in the long continuity of kindred lives, it does not lose itself in any power less gentle, less magical, less universal than itself, or less the enemy of cruelty; for what it finds is what it brings, and what it sees is what it is; and though the First Cause may be both good and evil, a Power has risen out of it against which all the evil in it and all the unthinkable atrocities it brings to pass are fighting a losing battle.

JOHN COWPER POWYS (1872–1963), *Autobiography*

Whatever is said, it must be admitted that there is something astounding about Christianity. 'That is because you were born in it,' men will say. Far from it; I resist it for this very reason, for fear that my advantage may bias me. But although I was born in it I cannot help finding Christianity astounding.

PASCAL, *Pensées*

HUMAN SOLIDARITY

Human Solidarity. There is consolation in finding that we are not alone, that others have wrestled with the same problems as we have; that others, even, have thought about themselves as much as we do, and found good reasons for doing so. Thus, even our self-preoccupation, our 'aloneness', is seen to make us securely a part of the human race.

How do others cope? From Yeats's stern formula to Ruskin on the value of detail, the matter here largely concerns techniques for living. From Goethe to Bacon, the discussion is also about techniques, with an examination of 'the uses of adversity', the role of chance, the possible benefits of suffering.

Peacock exalts the value of common-sense optimism in the face of fashionable gloom, with which Chesterton, Grigson, Goethe, Sydney Smith, Bellow concur, in their different ways. MacNeice even comes round to the truth in his father's truisms, which appear to him in the form of a blessing.

There follow experiences of blessing, expressions of gratitude, praise of heroes, evidence of human courage (Milton's 'steer right onward'), recognition of the nobility of 'ordinary' men and women, and celebration of the 'dailyness of life': 'To be happy at home,' says Dr Johnson, 'is the ultimate result of all ambition.' Gurney's hope lies in the love of small, unnoticed things, 'trifles', and Patrick Kavanagh insists that we should record that love 'without claptrap', which he does in the least promising of circumstances, the functional ward of a chest hospital: 'But nothing whatever is by love debarred.'

Nor dread nor hope attend
A dying animal;
A man awaits his end
Dreading and hoping all;
Many times he died,
Many times rose again.
A great man in his pride
Confronting murderous men
Casts derision upon
Supersession of breath;
He knows death to the bone –
Man has created death.

W. B. YEATS (1865–1939)

Know then thyself, presume not God to scan;
The proper study of mankind is man.
Placed on this isthmus of a middle state,
A being darkly wise, and rudely great:
With too much knowledge for the Sceptic side,
With too much weakness for the Stoic's pride,
He hangs between; in doubt to act, or rest,
In doubt to deem himself a god, or beast;
In doubt his mind or body to prefer;
Born but to die, and reasoning but to err;
Alike in ignorance, his reason such,
Whether he thinks too little, or too much;
Chaos of thought and passion, all confused;
Still by himself abused, or disabused;
Created half to rise, and half to fall;
Great lord of all things, yet a prey to all;
Sole judge of truth, in endless error hurled:
The glory, jest, and riddle of the world!

ALEXANDER POPE (1688–1744), from *An Essay on Man*

If everyone did not take such an excessive and exaggerated *interest in himself*, life would be so uninteresting that no one would put up with it.

SCHOPENHAUER (1788–1860)

And I say to mankind, Be not curious about God,
For I who am curious about each am not curious about God,
(No array of terms can say how much I am at peace about
  God and about death.)
I hear and behold God in every object, yet understand God
  not in the least,
Nor do I understand who there can be more wonderful than
  myself.

WALT WHITMAN (1819–92), from 'Song of Myself'

Had we not loved ourselves at all, we could never have been obliged to love anything. So that self-love is the basis of all love. But when we do love ourselves, and self-love is satisfied infinitely in all its desires and possible demands, then it is easily led to regard the Benefactor more than itself, and for his sake overflows abundantly to all others. So that God by satisfying my self-love, hath enabled and engaged me to love others.

THOMAS TRAHERNE (1637–74)

The motives of the best actions will not bear too strict an enquiry. It is allowed, that the cause of most actions, good or bad, may be resolved into the love of ourselves. But the self-love of some men inclines them to please others; and the self-love of others is wholly employed in pleasing themselves. This makes the great distinction between virtue and vice. Religion is the best motive of all actions, yet religion is allowed to be the highest instance of self-love.

JONATHAN SWIFT (1667–1745), *Thoughts on Various Subjects*

Do not be too much discouraged if any virtue be mixed in your consciousness with affectation and imperfect sincerity, or some vanity – disapprove of this – and continue the practice & the good feeling even thus mixed – it will gradually purify itself.

S. T. COLERIDGE (1772–1834), Notebooks

Practise, even when success looks hopeless. The left hand, inept in other respects for lack of practice, can grasp the reins more firmly than the right, because here it has had practice.

MARCUS AURELIUS (AD 121–180)

18 JULY 1827

My nerves have for these two or three last days been susceptible of an acute excitement from the slightest causes; the beauty of the evening, the sighing of the summer breeze, brings the tears into my eyes not unpleasingly. But I must take exercise, and caseharden myself. There is no use in encouraging these moods of the mind. It is not the law we live on.

24 SEPTEMBER 1827

Worked in the morning as usual, and sent off the proofs and copy. Something of the black dog still hanging about me; but I will shake him off. I generally affect good spirits in company of my family, whether I am enjoying them or not. It is too severe to sadden the harmless mirth of others by suffering your own causeless melancholy to be seen; and this species of exertion is, like virtue, its own reward; for the good spirits, which are at first simulated, become at length real.

10 MAY 1829

This must be a day of preparation, which I hate; yet it is but laying aside a few books, and arranging a few papers, and yet my nerves are fluttered, and I make blunders, and mislay my pen and my keys, and make more confusion than I can repair. After all, I will try for once to do it steadily.

Well! I have toiled through it; it is like a ground swell in the sea that brings up all that is disgusting from the bottom – admonitory letters – unpaid bills – few of these thank my stars!

– all that one would wish to forget perks itself up in your face at a thorough redding up – devil take it, I will get out and cool the fever that this turmoil has made in my veins! The delightful spring weather conjured down the evil spirit. I sat a long time with my nerves shaking like a frightened child, and then laughed at it all by the side of the river, coming back by the thicket.

SIR WALTER SCOTT (1771–1832), *Journals*

I know not what I should do without a Sunshiny morning now and then – it clears up one's spirits.

JOHN KEATS (1795–1821), from a letter

> We wasters of griefs!
> How we stare away into sad endurance beyond them,
> trying to foresee their end! – Whereas they are really
> seasons of us, our winter-
> outwearing leafage, meadows, ponds, inherited landscape,
> populated by rush-dwelling creatures and birds.

RILKE (1875–1926)

Dear Lady Georgiana,

 . . . Nobody has suffered more from low spirits than I have done – so I feel for you. 1st. Live as well as you dare. 2nd. Go into the shower-bath with a small quantity of water at a temperature low enough to give you a slight sensation of cold, 75° or 80°. 3rd. Amusing books. 4th. Short views of human life – not further than dinner or tea. 5th. Be as busy as you can. 6th. See as much as you can of those friends who respect and like you. 7th. And of those acquaintances who amuse you. 8th. Make no secret of low spirits to your friends, but talk of them freely – they are always worse for dignified concealment. 9th. Attend to the effects tea and coffee produce upon you. 10th. Compare your lot with that of other people. 11th. Don't expect too much from human life – a sorry business at the best. 12th. Avoid poetry, dramatic representations (except comedy), music, serious novels, melancholy sentimental people, and everything likely to excite feeling or emotion not ending in active benevolence. 13th. *Do good*, and endeavour to please everybody of every degree. 14th. Be as much as you can in the open air without fatigue. 15th. Make the room where you commonly sit, gay and pleasant. 16th. Struggle by little and little against idleness. 17th. Don't be too severe upon yourself, or underrate yourself, but do yourself justice. 18th. Keep good blazing fires. 19th. Be firm and constant in the exercise of rational religion. 20th. Believe me, dear Lady Georgiana,

Very truly yours,

SYDNEY SMITH (1771–1845)

William Cowper tells of the relief he found in *The Temple* when he was first 'overtaken with a dejection of spirits' at the age of 21:

> At length I met with Herbert's Poems; and gothic and uncouth as they were, I yet found in them a strain of piety which I could not but admire. This was the only author I had any delight in reading. I pored over him all day long; and though I found not here what I might have found – a cure for my malady, yet it never seemed so much alleviated as while I was reading him.

WILLIAM COWPER (1731–1800), *Memoirs*

Think that the grass upon thy grave is green;
   Think that thou seest thine own empty chair;
   The empty garments thou wast wont to wear
   The empty room where long thy haunt hath been:
Think that the lane, the meadow, and the wood
   And mountain summit feel thy foot no more,
   Nor the loud thoroughfare, nor sounding shore:
   All mere blank space where thou thyself hast stood.
Amid this thought-created silence say
   To thy stripped soul, what am I now and where?
   Then turn and face the petty narrowing care
Which has been gnawing thee for many a day,
   And it will die as dies a wailing breeze
   Lost in the solemn roar of boundless seas.

JAMES SMETHAM (1821–89)

Happiness

I have been happy for two years. It mayn't be over yet, but I want to write it down before it gets spoiled by pain – which is the chief thing pain can do in the inside life: spoil the lovely things that had got in there first.

Happiness can come in one's natural growth and not queerly, as religious people think. From 51 to 53 I have been happy, and would like to remind others that their turns can come too. It is the only message worth giving.

E. M. FORSTER (1879–1970), *Commonplace Book*

You perhaps at one time thought there was such a thing as Worldly Happiness to be arrived at, at certain periods of time marked out – you have of necessity from your disposition been thus led away – I scarcely remember counting upon any happiness – I look not for it if it be not in the present hour – nothing startles me beyond the moment. The setting sun will always set me to rights – or if a sparrow come before my window I take part in its existence and pick about the gravel.

JOHN KEATS, from a letter

[The imagination] is eminently a *weariable* faculty, eminently delicate, and incapable of bearing fatigue; so that if we give it too many objects at a time to employ itself upon, or very grand ones for a long time together, it fails under the effort, becomes jaded, exactly as the limbs do by bodily fatigue, and incapable of answering any farther appeal till it has had rest . . .

I well recollect the walk on which I first found out this; it was on the winding road from Sallenches, sloping up the hills towards St Gervais, one cloudless Sunday afternoon. The road circles softly between bits of rocky bank and mounded pasture; little cottages and chapels gleaming out from among the trees at every turn. Behind me, some leagues in length, rose the jagged range of the mountains of the Reposoir; on the other side of the valley, the mass of the Aiguille de Varens, heaving its seven thousand feet of cliff into the air at a single effort, its gentle gift of waterfall, the Nant d'Arpenaz, like a pillar of cloud at its feet; Mont Blanc and all its aiguilles, one silver flame, in front of me; marvellous blocks of mossy granite and dark glades of pine around me; but I could enjoy nothing, and could not for a long while make out what was the matter with me, until at last I discovered that if I confined myself to one thing, – and that a little thing, – a tuft of moss, or a single crag at the top of the Varens, or a wreath or two of foam at the bottom of the Nant d'Arpenaz, I began to enjoy it directly, because then I had mind enough to put into the thing, and the enjoyment arose from the quantity of the imaginative energy I could bring to bear upon it; but when I looked at or thought of all together, moss, stones, Varens, Nant d'Arpenaz, and Mont Blanc, I had not mind enough to give to all, and none were of any value. The conclusion which would have been formed, upon this, by a German philosopher, would have been that the Mont Blanc *was* of no value; that he and his imagination only were of value; that the Mont Blanc, in fact, except so far as he was able to look at it, could not be considered as having any existence. But the only conclusion which occurred to me as reasonable under the circumstances (I have seen no ground for altering it since) was, that I was an exceedingly small creature, much tired, and, at the moment, not a little stupid, for whom a blade of grass, or a wreath of foam, was quite food enough and to spare, and that if I tried to take any more, I should make myself ill. Whereupon, associating myself fraternally with some ants, who were deeply interested in the conveyance of some small sticks over the road, and rather, as I think they generally are, in too great a hurry about it, I returned home in a little while with great contentment; thinking how well it was ordered that, as Mont Blanc and his pine forests could not be everywhere, nor all the world come to see them, the human mind, on the whole, should enjoy itself most surely, in an antlike manner, and be happy and busy with the bits of sticks and grains of crystal that fall in its way to be handled, in daily duty.

JOHN RUSKIN (1819–1900), *Modern Painters*

Everything we do has a result. But that which is right and prudent does not always lead to good, nor the contrary to what is bad; frequently the reverse takes place. Some time since, I made a mistake in one of these transactions with booksellers, and was sorry that I had done so. But now circumstances have so altered, that, if I had not made that very mistake, I should have made a greater one. Such instances occur frequently in life, and hence we see men of the world, who know this, going to work with great freedom and boldness.

GOETHE (1749–1832), *Conversations*

Remember that chance, which (together with error its brother, folly its aunt, and wickedness its grandmother) is the ruling power on this earth and embitters the life of every son of earth, and yours as well, yearly and daily by blows great and small; – remember, I say, that it is this mischievous power to which you owe your well-being and independence, for it gave to you what it denied to many thousands, just to be able to give it to individuals like you. If you remember this, you will not act as though you had a right to the possession of that for which you are thanking it. On the contrary, you will know that you have all this through the favour of a fickle mistress. Therefore, when she is in the mood to take back from you some or all of these things, you will not raise a hue and cry about her injustice, but you will realize that chance took what chance had given. If needs be, you will observe that it is not quite so favourable to you as it hitherto seemed to be. Indeed, it could dispose not merely of what it had given, but also of what you had earned through hard work and honesty!

But now if chance is ever so favourable to you that it gives you much more than to almost all in whose footsteps you want to go, then be pleased, do not be eager for the possession of the gifts it has bestowed, do not make a wrong use of them, but regard them as property held from a capricious lord, and use them with wisdom and benevolence.

SCHOPENHAUER (1788–1860), *Early MSS*

Misfortune has its uses. It is good to be born in very depraved times; for, compared with others, you gain a reputation for virtue at a small cost.

MONTAIGNE (1533–92), 'On Presumption'

The lopped tree
  In time may grow again,
Most naked plants
  Renew both fruit and flower:
The sorriest wight
  May find release of pain,
The dryest soil
  Suck in some moistening shower.
Times go by turns,
  And chances change by course,
From foul to fair,
  From better hap to worse.

The sea of fortune
  Doth not ever flow,
She draws her favours
  To the lowest ebb;
Her tides have equal times
  To come and go,
Her loom doth weave
  The fine and coarsest web;
No joy so great,
  But runneth to an end:
No hap so hard
  But may in fine amend.

Not always fall of leaf,
  Nor ever Spring;
No endless night,
  Nor yet eternal day;
The saddest birds
  A season find to sing,
The roughest storm

A calm may soon allay.
Thus with succeeding turns
God tempereth all,
That man may hope to rise
Yet fear to fall.

A chance may win
That by mischance was lost;
That net that holds no great
Takes little fish;
In some things all,
In all things none are crossed:
Few all they need,
But none have all they wish.
Unmeddled joys
Here to no man befall:
Who least, has some,
Who most, hath never all.

ROBERT SOUTHWELL (*c.*1561–95),
'Times Go by Turns'

Imaginary grievances have always been more my torment than
real ones. You know this well. Real ones will never have any
other effect upon me than to stimulate me to get out of or avoid
them. This is easily accounted for. Our imaginary woes are
conjured up by our passions, and are fostered by passionate
feeling: our real ones come of themselves, and are opposed by
an abstract exertion of mind. Real grievances are displacers of
passion. The imaginary nail a man down for a sufferer, as on a
cross; the real spur him up into an agent.

JOHN KEATS, from a letter

As we ought not to give way to fear, any more than indulgence
to hope, because the objects both of fear and hope are yet
uncertain, so we ought not to trust the representations of one
more than of the other, because they are both equally fall-
acious; as hope enlarges happiness, fear aggravates calamity. It

is generally allowed, that no man ever found the happiness of possession proportionate to that expectation which incited his desire, and invigorated his pursuit; nor has any man found the evils of life so formidable in reality, as they are described to him by his own imagination: every species of distress brings with it some peculiar supports, some unforeseen means of resisting, or power of enduring. Taylor justly blames some pious persons, who indulge their fancies too much, set themselves, by the force of imagination, in the place of the ancient martyrs and confessors, and question the validity of their own faith, because they shrink at the thoughts of flames and tortures. It is, says he, sufficient that you are able to encounter the temptations which now assault you; when God sends trials, he may send strength.

SAMUEL JOHNSON (1709–84), The Rambler

Dear Sir,

I am returned from the annual ramble into the middle counties. Having seen nothing I had not seen before, I have nothing to relate. Time has left that part of the island few antiquities; and commerce has left the people no singularities. I was glad to go abroad, and, perhaps, glad to come home; which is, in other words, I was, I am afraid, weary of being at home, and weary of being abroad. Is not this the state of life? But, if we confess this weariness, let us not lament it; for all the wise and all the good say, that we may cure it.

For the black fumes which rise in your mind, I can prescribe nothing but that you disperse them by honest business or innocent pleasure, and by reading, sometimes easy and sometimes serious. Change of place is useful; and I hope that your residence at Auchinleck will have many good effects.

SAMUEL JOHNSON, from a letter to James Boswell

That thee is sent, receive in buxomness,
The wrestling for this world asketh a fall.
Here is no home, here is but wilderness.
Forth pilgrim, forth! Forth beast out of thy stall!
Know thy countrie, look up, thank God of all,
Hold the high way, and let thy ghost thee lead,
And truth thee shall deliver, it is no drede.

GEOFFREY CHAUCER (*c.*1343–1400),
from 'Le Bon Conseil de G. Chaucer'

If it should come to pass, and we found ourselves
Helplessly truthful – like someone in deep shock
Giving his first statement to the police
After the fatal accident: 'I swerved.'
'I took my eyes off him.' 'I thought I had time.' –

Or someone before doctors, describing his pains
With his best candour and his anxious eyes,
Undressing as instructed like a child
And after the examination going
Where he is told – if it should come to this

And we before authority should be bound
To tell the most complex truth in the simplest words
(Which the bench should have the skill to understand)
Then surely, after sentence, helplessly
Truthful, without pretence or anxiety,
We would take whatever fate, how nearly happily.

E. J. SCOVELL (*b.*1907), 'Judgement Day'

When I am at work, I feel an unlimited faith in art, and that I shall succeed, but in days of physical prostration, or when there are financial obstacles, I feel that faith diminishing, and a doubt overwhelms me, which I try to conquer by setting to work again at once. It is the same thing with the woman and the children; when I am with them, and the little chap comes creeping towards me on all fours, crowing for joy, I have not the slightest doubt that everything is right.

How often has that child comforted me.

When I am at home, he can't leave me alone for a moment; when I am at work, he pulls at my coat or climbs up against my leg, till I take him on my lap. In the studio, he crows at everything, plays quietly with a bit of paper, a bit of string, or an old brush; the child is always happy. If he keeps this temperament all his life, he will be cleverer than I am.

Now what shall we say about the fact that there are times when one feels there is a certain fatality, that makes the good turn out wrong, and the bad turn out well.

I think one may consider those thoughts partly as a consequence of overwrought nerves, and if one has them, one must not think it one's duty to believe that things are really as gloomy as one supposes; if one did so, it would make one mad. On the contrary, it is reasonable to strengthen one's physique then, and afterward set to work like a man, and if that does not help, *still one must always continue to use those two means*, and consider that melancholy as fatal. In the long run, one will then feel one's energy increase, and will bear up against the troubles. Mysteries remain, sorrow or melancholy remains, but that everlasting negative is balanced by the positive work which is thus achieved after all. If life were as simple, and things as little complicated as in the tale of Goody-Goody, or the hackneyed sermon of the average clergyman, it would not be so very difficult to make one's way. But it is not so, and things are infinitely more complicated, and right and wrong do not stand separate, any more than black and white do in nature. One must take care not to fall back upon opaque black, that is deliberate wrong; and still more, one has to avoid the whiteness of a whitewashed wall, which means hypocrisy and everlasting Pharisaism. He who tries courageously to follow reason, and especially conscience, the very highest reason – the sublime reason – and tries to remain honest, can scarcely altogether lose his way, I think, though he will not get off without mistakes, checks and disheartenments, and will not reach perfection.

And I think it will give him a deep feeling of pity and benevolence, broader than the narrow-mindedness which is the stock-in-trade of clergymen.

VINCENT VAN GOGH (1853–90), from a letter to his brother

This light and darkness in our chaos joined,
What shall divide? The God within the mind.
    Extremes in nature equal ends produce,
In Man they join to some mysterious use;
Tho' each by turns the other's bound invade,
As, in some well-wrought picture, light and shade,
And oft so mix, the difference is too nice
Where ends the virtue, or begins the vice.
    Fools! who from hence into the notion fall,
That Vice or Virtue there is none at all.
If white and black blend, soften, and unite
A thousand ways, is there no black or white?
Ask your own heart, and nothing is so plain;
'Tis to mistake them, costs the time and pain.

ALEXANDER POPE, from *An Essay on Man*

God made both black and white men
without saying which were better.
He sent them the same sorrows
beneath one and the same cross –
but he made light, also,
to show the difference between colours.

JOSÉ HERNANDEZ (1834–86),
from *Martín Fierro the Gaucho*

Flee luxury, flee enfeebling good fortune, from which men's minds grow sodden, and if nothing intervenes to remind them of the common lot, they sink, as it were, into the stupor of unending drunkenness. The man who has always had glazed windows to shield him from a draught, whose feet have been kept warm by hot applications renewed from time to time, whose dining-halls have been tempered by hot air passing beneath the floor and circulating round the walls, – this man will run great risk if he is brushed by a gentle breeze. While all excesses are hurtful, the most dangerous is unlimited good fortune. It excites the brain, it evokes vain fancies in the mind, and clouds in deep fog the boundary between falsehood and truth. Would it not be better, summoning virtue's help, to endure everlasting ill fortune than to be bursting with un-limited and immoderate blessings? Death from starvation comes very gently, but from gorging men explode.

SENECA (*c.*BC 4–65 AD), *On Providence*

Suffering is as necessary to our moral character as the pressure of the atmosphere is to our body. Without this the body would burst, and without suffering our character would plunge into all kinds of passions and sensual pleasures.

SCHOPENHAUER, *Early MSS*

But I don't want you to think I am rigidly opposed to Fortune, for there are times when she stops deceiving and helps man. I mean when she reveals herself, when she throws off her disguise and admits her game. Perhaps you still don't understand what I'm saying. What I want to say is a paradox, and so I am hardly able to put it into words. For bad fortune, I think, is more use to a man than good fortune. Good fortune always seems to bring happiness, but deceives you with her smiles, whereas bad fortune is always truthful because by changing she shows her true fickleness. Good fortune deceives, but bad fortune en-lightens. With her display of specious riches good fortune enslaves the minds of those who enjoy her, while bad fortune gives men release through the recognition of how fragile a thing happiness is. And so you can see Fortune in one way capricious, wayward and ever inconstant, and in another way sober, prepared and made wise by the experience of her own adver-sity. And lastly, by her flattery good fortune lures men away from the path of true good, but adverse fortune frequently draws men back to their true good like a shepherdess with her crook.

BOETHIUS (*c.*475–525), *Consolations of Philosophy*

For instance suppose a rose to have sensation, it blooms on a beautiful morning it enjoys itself – but there comes a cold wind, a hot sun – it cannot escape it, it cannot destroy its annoyances – they are as native to the world as itself: no more can man be happy in spite, the worldly elements will prey upon his nature – The common cognomen of this world among the misguided and superstitious is 'a vale of tears' from which we are to be redeemed by a certain arbitrary interposition of God and taken to Heaven – What a little circumscribed straightened notion! Call the world if you please 'The vale of Soul-making'. Then you will find out the use of the world (I am speaking now in the highest terms for human nature admitting it to be immortal which I will here take for granted for the purpose of showing a thought which has struck me concerning it). I say *'Soul making'* – Soul as distinguished from an Intelligence – There may be intelligences or sparks of the divinity in millions – but they are not Souls till they acquire identities, till each one is personally itself. Intelligences are atoms of perception – they know and they see and they are pure, in short they are God – How then are Souls to be made? How then are these sparks which are God to have identity given them – so as ever to possess a bliss peculiar to each one's individual existence? How, but by the medium of a world like this?

JOHN KEATS, from a letter

There can be no question of an antithesis between an optimistic and a pessimistic theory of life; only the simultaneous working together and against each other of both primordial drives, of Eros and the death drive, can explain the colourfulness of life, never the one or the other all by itself.

SIGMUND FREUD (1856–1939), *Analysis Terminable and Interminable*

It was a high speech of Seneca (after the manner of the Stoics), that *the good things which belong to prosperity are to be wished, but the good things that belong to adversity are to be admired.* Certainly if miracles be the command over nature, they appear most in adversity. It is yet a higher speech of his than the other (much too high for a heathen), *It is true greatness to have in one the frailty of a man and the security of a god.* This would have done better in poesy, where transcendencies are more allowed; and the poets indeed have been busy with it. For it is in effect the thing which is figured in that strange fiction of the ancient poets (which seemeth not to be without mystery, nay, and to have some approach to the state of a Christian), that Hercules, when he went to unbind Prometheus, by whom human nature is represented, sailed the length of the great ocean in an earthen pot or pitcher; lively describing Christian resolution, that saileth in the frail bark of the flesh through the waves of the world. But to speak in a mean, the virtue of prosperity is temperance, the virtue of adversity is fortitude, which in morals is the more heroical virtue. Prosperity is the blessing of the Old Testament, adversity is the blessing of the New, which carrieth the greater benediction, and the clearer revelation of God's favour. Yet, even in the Old Testament, if you listen to David's harp, you shall hear as many hearse-like airs as carols: and the pencil of the Holy Ghost hath laboured more in describing the afflictions of Job than the felicities of Solomon. Prosperity is not without many fears and distastes; and adversity is not without comforts and hopes. We see in needle-works and embroideries, it is more pleasing to have a lively work upon a sad and solemn ground, than to have a dark and melancholy work upon a lightsome ground: judge therefore of the pleasure of the heart by the pleasure of the eye. Certainly virtue is like precious odours, most fragrant when they are incensed or crushed; for prosperity doth best discover vice, but adversity doth best discover virtue.

FRANCIS BACON (1561–1626), 'Of Adversity'

THE HONOURABLE MR LISTLESS: Really I should like very well to lead such a life myself, but the exertion would be too much for me. Besides, I have been at college. I contrive to get through my day by sinking the morning in bed, and killing the evening in company; dressing and dining in the intermediate space, and stopping the chinks and crevices of the few vacant moments that remain with a little easy reading. And that amiable discontent and antisociality which you reprobate in our present drawing-room-table literature, I find, I do assure you, a very fine mental tonic, which reconciles me to my favourite pursuit of doing nothing, by showing me that nobody is worth doing any thing for.

MARIONETTA: But is there not in such compositions a kind of unconscious self-detection, which seems to carry their own antidote with them? For surely no one who cordially and truly either hates or despises the world will publish a volume every three months to say so.

MR FLOSKY: There is a secret in all this, which I will elucidate with a dusky remark. According to Berkeley, the *esse* of things is *percipi*. They exist as they are perceived. But, leaving for the present, as far as relates to the material world, the material-ists, hyloists, and antihyloists, to settle this point among them, which is indeed

> A subtle question, raised among
> Those out o' their wits, and those i' the wrong

for only we transcendalists are in the right: we may very safely assert that the *esse* of happiness is *percipi*. It exists as it is perceived. 'It is the mind that maketh well or ill.' The elements of pleasure and pain are every where. The degree of happiness that any circumstances or objects can confer on us depends on the mental disposition with which we approach them. If you consider what is meant by the common phrases, a happy disposition and a discontented temper, you will perceive that the truth for which I am contending is universally admitted.

(Mr Flosky suddenly stopped: he found himself unintentionally trespassing within the limits of common sense.)

MR HILARY: It is very true; a happy disposition finds materials of enjoyment every where. In the city, or the country – in society, or in solitude – in the theatre, or the forest – in the hum of the multitude, or in the silence of the mountains, are alike materials of reflection and elements of pleasure. It is one mode of pleasure to listen to the music of 'Don Giovanni', in a theatre glittering with light, and crowded with elegance and beauty: it is another to glide at sunset over the bosom of a lonely lake, where no sound disturbs the silence but the motion of the boat through the waters. A happy disposition derives pleasure from both, a discontented temper from neither, but is always busy in detecting deficiencies, and feeding dissatisfaction with comparisons. The one gathers all the flowers, the other all the nettles, in its path. The one has the faculty of enjoying every thing, the other of enjoying nothing. The one realises all the pleasure of the present good; the other converts it into pain, by pining after something better, which is only better because it is not present, and which, if it were present, would not be enjoyed. These morbid spirits are in life what professed critics are in literature; they see nothing but faults, because they are predetermined to shut their eyes to beauties. The critic does his utmost to blight genius in its infancy; that which rises in spite of him he will not see; and then he complains of the decline of literature. In like manner, these cankers of society complain of human nature and society, when they have wilfully debarred themselves from all the good they contain, and done their utmost to blight their own happiness and that of all around them. Misanthropy is sometimes the product of disappointed benevolence; but it is more frequently the offspring of overweening and mortified vanity, quarrelling with the world for not being better treated than it deserves.

SCYTHROP *(to Marionetta)*: These remarks are rather uncharitable. There is a great good in human nature, but it is at present ill-conditioned. Ardent spirits cannot but be dissatisfied with things as they are; and, according to their views of the probabilities of amelioration, they will rush into the extremes of either hope or despair – of which the first is enthusiasm, and the second misanthropy; but their sources in this case are the same, as the Severn and the Wye run in different directions, and both rise in Plinlimmon.

MARIONETTA: 'And there is salmon in both'; for the resemblance is about as close as that between Macedon and Monmouth.

THOMAS LOVE PEACOCK (1785–1866), *Nightmare Abbey*

There is danger in that modern phrase 'divine discontent'. There is truth in it also, of course; but it is only truth of a special and secondary kind. Much of the quarrel between Christianity and the world has been due to this fact; that there are generally two truths, as it were, at any given moment of revolt or reaction, and the ancient underlying truism which is nevertheless true all the time. It is sometimes worth while to point out that black is not so black as it is painted; but black is still black, and not white. So with the merits of content and discontent. It is true that in certain acute and painful crises of oppression or disgrace, discontent is a duty and shame should call us like a trumpet. But it is not true that man should look at life with an eye of discontent, however high-minded. It is not true that in his primary, naked relation to the world, in his relation to sex, to pain, to comradeship, to the grave or to the weather, man ought to make discontent his ideal; it is black lunacy. Half his poor little hopes of happiness hang on his thinking a small house pretty, a plain wife charming, a lame foot not unbearable, and bad cards not so bad. The voice of the special rebels and prophets, recommending discontent, should, as I have said, sound now and then suddenly, like a trumpet. But the voices of the saints and sages, recommending contentment, should sound unceasingly, like the sea.

G. K. CHESTERTON (1874–1936), 'What Is Right with the World'

Last winter, I think last spring as well, hardly a night's television news went by – on screens fed by the BBC – without the flames, somewhere, in some city in Great Britain, some store, some warehouse, of a large destructive fire. I wouldn't suppose there were in fact more fires at that time than there are usually, but I used to wait for the night's fire: it was as if all England were burning, it was a disproportionate offering several times a week (I don't think I exaggerate) of ordinary inevitable accident; it was as if no visual bulletin could be complete without alarm and fear. In a small way, yet reaching to millions, this nightly fire was rather like the parading of hell fire and damnation in earlier ages, or among particular religious communities, like paintings of the red mouth of Hell and the Last Judgment. A perverse enjoyment, perhaps; which is not the enjoyment I am asking for, and asking that no individual should be afraid of admitting to himself or to others.

I am myself – like most of our community in these islands – no religionist. But it happens that I was born in the best room of a vicarage (facing south, over dahlias) and brought up in a vicarage, so I shall go back for a moment to that medieval Christian image of the gaping red gullet of Hell, in the shape of Leviathan, with flames, and large teeth, and an insatiable greed for sinners. In a book which came out last year, on images of Heaven and Hell in western Art, I read of a German theologian of the sixteenth century, I suppose of the Counter Reformation, named Drexelius, who maintained that the deity found no difficulty at all in cramming one hundred thousand million souls of the burnt, the skinned and the gutted – the damned in brief – into one cubic German mile. Little cause for felicity or for enjoying things if that was your belief, and if yourself might be burned, skinned, gutted, by demons. But then I had only to go through that book to be reminded that the medieval artist and believer was also in the habit of balancing Hell with Heaven in the same picture, or the same painting on a church wall. There, like Osiris before him, St Michael the Archangel held up the scales, and weighed the souls of the dead. If devils, on one side of the picture, at once clawed into Leviathan's flaming mouth the souls of those whose evil outweighed their goodness, at least on the other side souls of the proper weight were received gently and happily into bliss. So a Last Judgment preserved more or less the open situation, devoid of an excluding fanaticism, or of a morbid preferred insistence on hell and torture and gloom; and I am asking for an open situation, a balance in our own life of the mind: perhaps not a balance, but at any rate an oscillation, corresponding to reality.

We are not each of us – I don't speak just as a writer – called upon by decency or kindness or moral imagination or necessity or the inescapable facts or the universal weight and posture of things, to suppose all the time that we are having to wade, companions of Thomas the Rhymer in the border ballad, through red blude to the knee, seeing neither sun nor moon but only the glare of the burning of napalm on innocent bodies. The evil is evil; in any case, unpalatable fact, we do each and all of us have to die sooner or later. Even then it is proper, surely, to criticize and correct ourselves either way: we need to see the detestable and the enjoyable with equal vision.

GEOFFREY GRIGSON (1905–85), 'Poems and Pleasure'

Goethe spoke of a new article in the *Edinburgh Review*. 'It is a pleasure to me,' said he, 'to see the elevation and excellence to which the English critics now rise. There is not a trace of their former pedantry, but its place is occupied by great qualities. In the last article – the one on German literature – you will find the following remarks: – "There are people among poets who have a tendency always to occupy themselves with things which another likes to drive from his mind." What say you to this? There we know at once where we are, and how we have to classify a great number of our most modern literati.'

GOETHE, *Conversations*

I certainly, my dear Jeffrey . . . do protest against your increasing and unprofitable scepticism. I exhort you to restrain the violent tendency of your nature for analysis, and to cultivate synthetical propensities. What's the use of virtue? What's the use of wealth? What's the use of honor? What's a guinea but a damned yellow circle? What's a chamber-pot but an infernal hollow sphere? The whole effort of your mind is to destroy. Because others build slightly and eagerly, you employ yourself in kicking down their houses, and contract a sort of aversion for the more honorable useful and difficult task of building well yourself.

SYDNEY SMITH

Everybody was in on the act. 'History' gave everyone a free ride. The very Himmelsteins who had never even read a book of metaphysics, were touching the Void, as if it were so much saleable real estate. This little demon was impregnated with modern ideas, and one in particular excited his terrible little heart: You must sacrifice your poor, squawking, niggardly individuality – which may be nothing anyway (from an analytic point of view) but a persistent infantile megalomania, or (from a Marxian point of view) a stinking little bourgeois property – to historical necessity. And to truth. And truth is true only as it brings down more disgrace and dreariness upon human beings, so that if it shows anything but evil it is an illusion, and not truth.

SAUL BELLOW (*b*.1915), *Herzog*

His father gave him a box of truisms
Shaped like a coffin, then his father died;
The truisms remained on the mantelpiece
As wooden as the playbox they had been packed in
Or that other his father skulked inside.

Then he left home, left the truisms behind him
Still on the mantelpiece, met love, met war,
Sordor, disappointment, defeat, betrayal,
Till through disbeliefs he arrived at a house
He could not remember seeing before,

And he walked straight in; it was where he had come from
And something told him the way to behave.
He raised his hand and blessed his home;
The truisms flew and perched on his shoulders
And a tall tree sprouted from his father's grave.

LOUIS MACNEICE (1907–63), 'The Truisms'

My Self. A living man is blind and drinks his drop.
  What matter if the ditches are impure?
  What matter if I live it all once more?
  Endure that toil of growing up;
  The ignominy of boyhood; the distress
  Of boyhood changing into man;
  The unfinished man and his pain
  Brought face to face with his own clumsiness;

The finished man among his enemies? –
How in the name of Heaven can he escape
That defiling and disfigured shape
The mirror of malicious eyes
Casts upon his eyes until at last
He thinks that shape must be his shape?
And what's the good of an escape
If honour find him in the wintry blast?

I am content to live it all again
And yet again, if it be life to pitch
Into the frog-spawn of a blind man's ditch,
A blind man battering blind men;
Or into that most fecund ditch of all,
The folly that man does
Or must suffer, if he woos
A proud woman not kindred of his soul.

I am content to follow to its source
Every event in action or in thought;
Measure the lot; forgive myself the lot!
When such as I cast out remorse
So great a sweetness flows into the breast
We must laugh and we must sing,
We are blest by everything,
Everything we look upon is blest.

W. B. YEATS, from 'A Dialogue of Self and Soul'

Alexandros appeared with a rag, a shoe brush and a big rusty knife; he got down on his knees and began manicuring my shoes. I was not in the least embarrassed. I thought to myself let him do as he likes, it gives him pleasure. I wondered vaguely what I might do myself to make men realize what great happiness lies in store for all of us. I sent out a benediction in every direction – to old and young, to the neglected savages in the forgotten parts of the earth, to wild as well as domesticated animals, to the birds of the air, to creeping things, to trees and plants and flowers, to rocks and lakes and mountains. This is the first day of my life, said I to myself, that I have included everybody and everything on this earth in one thought. I bless the world, every inch of it, every living atom, and it is all alive, breathing like myself, and conscious through and through.

HENRY MILLER (1891–1980), *The Colossus of Maroussi*

I have braved, for want of wild beasts, steel cages,
carved my term and nickname on bunks and rafters,
lived by the sea, flashed aces in an oasis,
dined with the-devil-knows-whom, in tails, on truffles.
From the height of a glacier I beheld half a world, the
   earthly
width. Twice have drowned, thrice let knives rake my nitty-
   gritty.
Quit the country that bore and nursed me.
Those who forgot me would make a city.
I have waded the steppes that saw yelling Huns in saddles,
worn the clothes nowadays back in fashion in every quarter,
planted rye, tarred the roofs of pigsties and stables,
guzzled everything save dry water.
I've admitted the sentries' third eye into my wet and foul
dreams. Munched the bread of exile: it's stale and warty.
Granted my lungs all sounds except the howl;
switched to a whisper. Now I am forty.
What should I say about life? That it's long and abhors
   transparence.
Broken eggs make me grieve; the omelette, though, makes
   me vomit.
Yet until brown clay has been crammed down my larynx,
only gratitude will be gushing from it.

JOSEPH BRODSKY (*b.*1940), 'May 24th, 1980'

I understand the large hearts of heroes,
The courage of present times and all times,
How the skipper saw the crowded and rudderless wreck of
    the steam-ship, and Death chasing it up and down the
    storm,
How he knuckled tight and gave not back an inch, and was
    faithful of days and faithful of nights,
And chalked in large letters on a board, *Be of good cheer,*
    we will not desert you;
How he followed with them and tacked with them three days
    and would not give it up,
How he saved the drifting company at last,
How the lank loose-gowned women looked when boated
    from the side of their prepared graves,
How the silent old-faced infants and the lifted sick, and the
    sharp-lipped unshaved men;
All this I swallow, it tastes good, I like it well, it becomes
    mine,
I am the man, I suffered, I was there.

WALT WHITMAN, from 'Song of Myself'

(THE COUNTER-TURN)
. . . Alas, but Morison fell young:
He never fell, thou fall'st, my tongue.
He stood, a soldier to the last right end,
A perfect patriot, and a noble friend,
But most a virtuous son.
All offices were done
By him, so ample full, and round,
In weight, in measure, number, sound,
As, though his age imperfect might appear,
His life was of humanity the sphere.

(THE STAND)
Go now, and tell out days summed up with fears,
And make them years;
Produce thy mass of miseries on the stage,
To swell thine age:

Repeat of things a throng,
To show thou hast been long,
Not lived; for life doth her great actions spell,
By what was done and wrought
In season, and so brought
To light: her measures are, how well
Each syllabe answered, and was formed how fair;
These make the lines of life, and that's her air.

(THE TURN)
It is not growing like a tree
In bulk, doth make man better be;
Or standing long an oak, three hundred year,
To fall a log at last, dry, bald, and sere:
A lily of a day
Is fairer far, in May,
Although it fall, and die that night;
It was the plant, and flower of light.
In small proportions, we just beauties see:
And in short measures, life may perfect be.

    BEN JONSON (1573–1637), from 'To the Immortal Memory and
Friendship of that Noble Pair, Sir Lucius Cary and Sir H. Morison'

Cyriack, this three years' day these eyes, though clear
To outward view, of blemish or of spot,
Bereft of light their seeing have forgot,
Nor to their idle orbs doth sight appear
Of sun or moon or star throughout the year,
Or man or woman. Yet I argue not
Against heaven's hand or will, nor bate a jot
Of heart or hope; but still bear up and steer
Right onward. What supports me doth thou ask?
The conscience, friend, to have lost them overplied
In liberty's defence, my noble task,
Of which all Europe talks from side to side.
This thought might lead me through the world's vain mask
Content though blind, had I no better guide.

JOHN MILTON (1608–74), 'To Mr Cyriack Skinner, Upon His Blindness'

We perceive no beauties that are not sharpened, prinked out, and inflated by artifice. Such as appear in their pure and natural simplicity easily escape a vision as coarse as ours. Theirs is a delicate and hidden beauty; it needs a clear and purified sight to discover their secret brightness. Is not simplicity, according to us, akin to foolishness and an object of scorn? Socrates sets his mind working with a natural and ordinary motion. A peasant says this, a woman says that. His talk is always of carters, joiners, cobblers, and masons. His inductions and comparisons are drawn from the commonest and most familiar actions of men; everyone understands him. Under so humble a form we should never have recognized the nobility and splendour of his admirable ideas – we who regard as low and dull all that are not embellished by learning, and who recognize riches only in pomp and show. Our world is fashioned solely for ostentation; men only puff themselves up with wind, and leap here and there, like balls. Socrates' purpose was not vain and fanciful; it was to provide us with matter and precepts that are of real and very direct service to life,

> *servare modum, finemque tenere,*
> *naturamque sequi.**

He was, moreover, always one and the same, and raised himself not spasmodically but by temperament to his highest efforts. Or, to put it better, he raised nothing, but rather brought down, reduced, and subjected all strength, obstacles, and difficulties to his own proper and natural level. In the case of Cato we can most clearly see that his pace is strained far beyond that of common men; in the brave exploits of his life and in his death, we always feel that he is mounted on a high horse. But Socrates moves close to the ground and, at a gentle and ordinary pace, discourses on the most useful subjects; and, when confronted with death and with the thorniest obstacles he could meet with, he follows the ordinary course of human life.

It is fortunate that the man who best deserves to be known

---

* To preserve the mean, pursue one's aim, and follow nature.

and presented as an example to the world should be the one of whom we have the most certain knowledge. He has been revealed in a clear light by the most clear-sighted men who ever lived; the accounts that we have of him are admirable both for their fidelity and their fullness. What a great thing it is that he was able to impart such order to thoughts as simple as a child's; without straining or altering them, he drew from them the most beautiful effects possible to the human mind. He does not display this in a rich or elevated, but merely in a healthy state, yet assuredly its health is both sound and vigorous.

By these common and natural means, by these ordinary and familiar ideas, without exciting or pricking himself on, he expounded not only the most regular, but also the most exalted and vigorous beliefs, actions, and morals that ever were. It is he who brought human wisdom down again from the skies where it was wasting its labour, and restored it to man, with whom its most normal, its most toilsome, and its most useful business lies.

Hear him pleading before his judges. See with what reasons he rouses his courage in the hazards of war, with what arguments he strengthens his patience against calumny, tyranny, death, and against his wife's temper. There is nothing borrowed from art and learning; the simplest may here recognize their own powers and strength; it is impossible to mount higher or to drop lower. He has done human nature a great kindness by showing it how much it can do of itself.

MONTAIGNE, 'On Physiognomy'

Is there, for honest poverty
   That hangs his head, and a' that;
The coward-slave, we pass him by,
   We dare be poor for a' that!
For a' that, and a' that,
   Our toils obscure, and a' that,
The rank is but the guinea's stamp,
   The man's the gowd for a' that.   gold

What though on hamely fare we dine,
    Wear hoddin grey, and a' that;   *coarse wool*
Gie fools their silks, and knaves their wine,
    A man's a man for 'a that:
For a' that, and a' that,
    Their tinsel show, and a' that;
The honest man, though e'er sae poor,
    Is king o' men for a' that.

Ye see yon birkie, ca'd a lord,   *fellow*
    Wha struts, and stares, and a' that;
Though hundreds worship at his word,
    He's but a coof for a' that: *fool*
For a' that, and a' that,
    His ribband, star, and a' that,
The man of independent mind,
    He looks and laughs at a' that.

A prince can mak a belted knight,
    A marquis, duke, and a' that:
But an honest man's aboon his might,   *above*
    Gude faith he mauna fa' that!   *must not try*
For a' that, and a' that,
    Their dignities, and a' that,
The pith o' sense, and pride o' worth,
    Are higher ranks than a' that.

Then let us pray that come it may,
    As come it will for a' that,
That sense and worth, o'er a' the earth,
    May bear the gree, and a' that.   *have the*
For a' that, and a' that,   *first place*
    It's comin yet for a' that,
That man to man, the warld o'er,
    Shall brothers be for a' that.

ROBERT BURNS (1759–96)

The old Man still stood talking by my side;
But now his voice to me was like a stream
Scarce heard; nor word from word could I divide;
And the whole body of the Man did seem
Like one whom I had met with in a dream;
Or like a man from some far region sent,
To give me human strength, by apt admonishment.

My former thoughts returned: the fear that kills;
And hope that is unwilling to be fed;
Cold, pain, and labour, and all fleshly ills;
And mighty Poets in their misery dead.
– Perplexed, and longing to be comforted,
My question eagerly did I renew,
'How is it that you live, and what is it you do?'

He with a smile did then his words repeat;
And said that, gathering leeches, far and wide
He travelled; stirring thus about his feet
The waters of the pools where they abide.
'Once I could meet with them on every side;
But they have dwindled long by slow decay;
Yet still I persevere, and find them where I may.'

While he was talking thus, the lonely place,
The old Man's shape, and speech – all troubled me:
In my mind's eye I seemed to see him pace
About the weary moors continually,
Wandering about alone and silently.
While I these thoughts within myself pursued,
He, having made a pause, the same discourse renewed.

And soon with this he other matter blended,
Cheerfully uttered, with demeanour kind,
But stately in the main; and, when he ended,
I could have laughed myself to scorn to find
In that decrepit Man so firm a mind.
'God,' said I, 'be my help and stay secure;
I'll think of the Leech-gatherer on the lonely moor!'

WILLIAM WORDSWORTH (1770–1850),
from 'Resolution and Independence'

The main of life is, indeed, composed of small incidents and petty occurrences; of wishes for objects not remote, and grief for disappointments of no fatal consequence; of insect vexations which sting us and fly away, impertinences which buzz awhile about us, and are heard no more; of meteorous pleasures which dance before us and are dissipated; of compliments which glide off the soul like other music, and are forgotten by him that gave, and him that received them.

Such is the general heap out of which every man is to cull his own condition: for, as the chemists tell us, that all bodies are resolvable into the same elements, and that the boundless variety of things arises from the different proportions of very few ingredients; so a few pains and a few pleasures are all the materials of human life, and of these the proportions are partly allotted by Providence, and partly left to the arrangement of reason and of choice.

As these are well or ill disposed, man is for the most part happy or miserable. For very few are involved in great events, or have their thread of life entwisted with the chain of causes on which armies or nations are suspended; and even those who seem wholly busied in public affairs, and elevated above low cares, or trivial pleasures, pass the chief part of their time in familiar and domestic scenes; from these they came into public life, to these they are every hour recalled by passions not to be suppressed; in these they have the reward of their toils, and to these at last they retire.

The great end of prudence is to give cheerfulness to those hours, which splendour cannot gild, and acclamation cannot exhilarate; those soft intervals of unbended amusement, in which a man shrinks to his natural dimensions, and throws aside the ornaments or disguises, which he feels in privacy to be useless incumbrances, and to lose all effect when they become familiar. To be happy at home is the ultimate result of all ambition, the end to which every enterprise and labour tends, and of which every desire prompts the prosecution.

SAMUEL JOHNSON, *The Rambler*

The institution of the family is to be commended for precisely the same reasons that the institution of the nation, or the institution of the city, are in this matter to be commended. It is a good thing for a man to live in a family for the same reason that it is a good thing for a man to be besieged in a city. It is a good thing for a man to live in a family in the same sense that it is a beautiful and delightful thing for a man to be snowed up in a street. They all force him to realize that life is not a thing from outside, but a thing from inside. Above all, they all insist upon the fact that life, if it be a truly stimulating and fascinating life, is a thing which, of its nature, exists in spite of ourselves. The modern writers who have suggested, in a more or less open manner, that the family is a bad institution, have generally confined themselves to suggesting, with much sharpness, bitterness, or pathos, that perhaps the family is not always very congenial. Of course the family is a good institution because it is uncongenial. It is wholesome precisely because it contains so many divergencies and varieties. It is, as the sentimentalists say, like a little kingdom, and, like most other little kingdoms, is generally in a state of something resembling anarchy. It is exactly because our brother George is not interested in our religious difficulties, but is interested in the Trocadero Restaurant, that the family has some of the bracing qualities of the commonwealth. It is precisely because our uncle Henry does not approve of the theatrical ambitions of our sister Sarah that the family is like humanity. The men and women who, for good reasons and bad, revolt against the family, are, for good reasons and bad, simply revolting against mankind. Aunt Elizabeth is unreasonable, like mankind. Papa is excitable, like mankind. Our youngest brother is mischievous, like mankind. Grandpapa is stupid like the world; he is old, like the world.

Those who wish, rightly or wrongly, to step out of all this, do definitely wish to step into a narrower world. They are dismayed and terrified by the largeness and variety of the family. Sarah wishes to find a world wholly consisting of private theatricals; George wishes to think the Trocadero a cosmos. I do not say, for a moment, that the flight to this narrower life may not be the right thing for the individual, any more than I say the same thing about flight into a monastery. But I do say that anything is bad and artificial which tends to make these people succumb to the strange delusion that they are stepping into a world which is actually larger and more varied than their own. The best way that a man could test his readiness to encounter the common variety of mankind would be to climb down a chimney into any house at random, and get on as well as possible with the people inside. And that is essentially what each one of us did on the day that he was born.

G. K. CHESTERTON, *Heretics*

How lovely the elder brother's
Life all laced in the other's,
Lóve-laced! – what once I well
Witnessed; so fortune fell.
When Shrovetide, two years gone,
Our boys' plays brought on
Part was picked for John,
Young Jóhn; then fear, then joy
Ran revel in the elder boy.
Now the night come, all
Our company thronged the hall;
Henry, by the wall,
Beckoned me beside him:
I came where called, and eyed him
By meanwhiles; making mý play
Turn most on tender byplay.
For, wrung all on love's rack
My lad, and lost in Jack,
Smiled, blushed, and bit his lip;
Or drove, with a diver's dip,
Clutched hands through claspèd knees;
And many a mark like these
Told tales with what heart's stress
He hung on the imp's success.
Now the other was bráss-bóld:
Hé had no work to hold
His heart up at the strain;

Nay, roguish ran the vein.
Two tedious acts were past;
Jack's call and cue at last;
When Henry, heart-forsook,
Dropped eyes and dared not look.
Thére! the háll rúng!
Dog, he did give tongue!
But Harry – in his hands he has flung
His tear-tricked cheeks of flame
For fond love and for shame.
    Ah Nature, framed in fault,
There's comfort then, there's salt;
Nature, bad, base, and blind,
Dearly thou canst be kind;
There dearly thén, deárly,
Dearly thou canst be kind.

GERARD MANLEY HOPKINS (1844–89), 'Brothers'

Her blood so well mixed and flesh so well pasted,
That though her youth faded her comeliness lasted,
The blue was worn off but the plum was well tasted.

Less smooth than her skin, and less white than her breast,
Was this polished stone beneath which she lies pressed;
Stop, reader, and sigh, while thou think'st on the rest.

With a just trim of virtue her soul was endued,
Not affectedly pious nor secretly lewd,
She cut even between the coquette and the prude.

And her will with her duty so equally stood
That, seldom opposed, she was commonly good,
And did pretty well, doing just what she would.

Declining all power, she found means to persuade,
Was then most regarded when most she obeyed,
The mistress in truth, when she seemed but the maid.

Such care of her own proper actions she took,
That on other folks' lives she had no time to look,
So censure and praise were struck out of her book;

Her thought still confined to its own little sphere,
She minded not who did excel or did err,
But just as the matter related to her;

Then too when her private tribunal was reared,
Her mercy so mixed with her judgement appeared
That her foes were condemned and her friends always
    cleared.

Her religion so well with her learning did suit
That in practice sincere, and in controverse mute,
She showed she knew better to live than dispute.

Some parts of the Bible by heart she recited,
And much in historical chapters delighted,
But in points about faith she was something short-sighted;

So notions and modes she referred to the schools,
And in matters of conscience adhered to two rules –
To advise with no bigots, and jest with no fools;

And scrupling but little, enough she believed;
By charity ample small sins she retrieved,
And when she had new clothes she always received.

Thus still whilst her morning unseen fled away
In ordering the linen, and making the tea,
That she scarce could have time for the Psalms of the day;

And while after dinner the night came so soon
That half she proposed very seldom was done,
With twenty 'God bless me's, how this day is gone!';

While she read and accounted and paid and abated,
Ate and drank, played and worked, laughed and cried, loved
   and hated,
As answered the end of her being created;

In the midst of her age came a cruel disease,
Which neither her broths nor receipts could appease,
So down dropped her clay; may her soul be at peace.

Retire from this sepulchre all the profane,
Ye that love for debauch or that marry for gain,
Retire lest ye trouble the *manes* of Jane.

But thou, that know'st love above interest or lust,
Strew the myrtle and rose on this once beloved dust,
And shed one pious tear upon Jinny the Just.

           MATTHEW PRIOR (1664–1721), from 'Jinny the Just'

      Job Davies, eighty-five
      Winters old, and still alive
      After the slow poison
      And treachery of the seasons.

      Miserable? Kick my arse!
      It needs more than the rain's hearse,
      Wind-drawn, to pull me off
      The great perch of my laugh.

      What's living but courage?
      Paunch full of hot porridge,
      Nerves strengthened with tea.
      Peat-black, dawn found me

      Mowing where the grass grew,
      Bearded with golden dew.
      Rhythm of the long scythe
      Kept this tall frame lithe.

What to do? Stay green.
Never mind the machine,
Whose fuel is human souls.
Live large, man, and dream small.

R. S. THOMAS (*b*.1913), 'Lore'

Elizabeth Pritchard, Elizabeth Pritchard, Liz,
We never know whom we shall miss.
Some deaths leave a gap that heals over
But others leave presences.

Last summer I teased when you filled every corner
With jugs of wild grasses
And froze to a statue under our tentative swallows.
But later when scything the grasses
It was your everywhere reverent vases
I saw, not the rankness I cut.
And in bird-empty wind when I walk on the swallows'
    messes
Crusting the floor of the shed still, even in winter,
It is never the birds I remember
But you, Elizabeth.

Even the pebbles you put to guard willow-herb seedlings
I find that I nod to, whether I want them or not,
As though the degree of your care for the small and
    abandoned
And tentative lingers, a seedling you planted.

You, who called yourself dotty, a typical dotty lone woman,
Unlucky in love, and I half-agreed and agree;
Though Elizabeth Pritchard,
Still puzzled and not understanding
Enough, when I think how I'd like to
Swing you up high to the mirror,
As grown-ups with children, a hand under each elbow,
To show you, triumphant; too late now,
The presence you are,
It is you that holds me.

P. J. KAVANAGH (*b*.1931), 'Late Acknowledgement'

I believe in the increasing of life: whatever
Leads to the seeing of small trifles,
Real, beautiful, is good; and an act never
Is worthier than in freeing spirit that stifles
Under ingratitude's weight, nor is anything done
Wiselier than the moving or breaking to sight
Of a thing hidden under by custom – revealed,
Fulfilled, used (sound-fashioned) any way out to delight:
Trefoil – hedge sparrow – the stars on the edge at night.

IVOR GURNEY (1890–1937), 'The Escape'

A year ago I fell in love with the functional ward
Of a chest hospital: square cubicles in a row
Plain concrete, wash basins – an art lover's woe,
Not counting how the fellow in the next bed snored.
But nothing whatever is by love debarred,
The common and banal her heat can know.
The corridor led to a stairway and below
Was the inexhaustible adventure of a gravelled yard.

This is what love does to things: the Rialto Bridge,
The main gate that was bent by a heavy lorry,
The seat at the back of a shed that was a suntrap.
Naming these things is the love-act and its pledge;
For we must record love's mystery without claptrap,
Snatch out of time the passionate transitory.

PATRICK KAVANAGH (1905–67), 'The Hospital'

PERSONAL FAITH

Personal faith: which does not depend specifically, although there are exceptions, on doctrinal Christianity. Swift considers death; and providence, which is Christianity with a small p. Pope is as stoic as a Stoic, and the ancients have their say on the matter. Boswell and Johnson converse on the physical nature of possible survival, and Donne puts in a charming plea for the necessity of bodies in heaven. These last are Christian, but have something distinctly 'personal' about them, as does Julian of Norwich, included here because her vision is almost domestic.

William Hazlitt offers the kind of consolation which is not uncommon, that we only fear death if we over-value life. This cold comfort is rejected by Thornton Wilder.

In a group of letters of condolence, Sydney Smith seems to take the Hazlitt line, in what is almost an aside, about it being better never to have been born. But such letters are difficult to write – necessary because, like social life, they 'promote kindness', and perhaps he was trying to enter and match the misery of his correspondent. Sir Walter Ralegh feels able to do this, to console philosophically, in 1597, but in 1618, after the death of their son, he admits heartbrokenly to his wife that until now he hadn't known what he was talking about. (Emily Dickinson's difficult letter is a little masterpiece of advance and retreat on this subject.)

W. H. Hudson describes being consoled by his mother, and thereafter the whole matter is thrown open to debate by various voices. This grouping was always going to turn into a noisy discussion, and one likely to tip over the border of sanity (Nijinsky) – called to order by Tennyson.

Despite what Blake says about external systems, we seem to need them, search for them, even if we shouldn't. Weil disposes of a new one, Freud's; D. H. Lawrence ponders 'a principle in the universe', Wordsworth asserts one; and, after Bishop Blougram's casuistry – 'What have we gained then by our unbelief . . .' – there follows a little group of what might be called 'creative atheism', the triumph of reason perhaps, another system which Blake defies.

It is impossible that anything so natural, so necessary, and so universal as death, should ever have been designed by providence as an evil to mankind.

JONATHAN SWIFT (1667–1745), 'Thoughts on Religion'

When a smart fit of sickness tells me this scurvy tenement of my body will fall in a little time, I am e'en as unconcerned as was that honest Hibernian, who being in bed in the great storm some years ago, and told the house would tumble over his head, made answer, What care I for the house? I am only a lodger.

ALEXANDER POPE (1688–1744), from a letter

As long as we remain within these bodily frames of ours, we are undergoing a heavy labour imposed on us by fate. For our human souls have come into our bodies from heaven: they have been sent down from their lofty abode and plunged, so to speak, into the earth, which is alien to their divine and eternal nature. As I believe, the reason why the immortal gods implanted souls in human beings was to provide the earth with guardians who should reflect their contemplation of the divine order in the orderly discipline of their own lives.

My own powers of logic and reasoning have not brought me to this conviction unaided. I have also relied upon the weighty and authoritative guidance of outstanding thinkers. For Pythagoras and his disciples – practically compatriots of ours, since they were known as the 'Italian philosophers' – never doubted, I am told, that each of our souls is a fraction taken from the divine universal Mind. Besides, I have studied the arguments concerning the immortality of the soul which Socrates advanced on the last day of his life; and he was the man whom the oracle of Apollo had pronounced to be wiser than all others.

CICERO (106–43 BC), *On Old Age*

Death is one of two things. Either it is annihilation, and the dead have no consciousness of anything; or, as we are told, it is really a change: a migration of the soul from this place to another. Now if there is no consciousness but only a dreamless sleep, death must be a marvellous gain. I suppose that if anyone were told to pick out the night on which he slept so soundly as not even to dream, and then to compare it with all the other nights and days of his life, and then were told to say, after due consideration, how many better and happier days and nights than this he had spent in the course of his life – well, I think that the Great King himself, to say nothing of any private person, would find these days and nights easy to count in comparison with the rest. If death is like this, then, I call it gain; because the whole of time, if you look at it in this way, can be regarded as no more than one single night. If on the other hand death is a removal from here to some other place, and if what we are told is true, that all the dead are there, what greater blessing could there be than this, gentlemen? If on arrival in the other world, beyond the reach of our so-called justice, one will find there the true judges who are said to preside in those courts, Minos and Rhadamanthys and Aeacus and Triptolemus and all those other half-divinities who were upright in their earthly life, would that be an unrewarding journey? Put it in this way: how much would one of you give to meet Orpheus and Musaeus, Hesiod and Homer? I am willing to die ten times over if this account is true.

PLATO (*c*.428–*c*.348 BC), *Apology of Socrates*

BOSWELL. 'One of the most pleasing thoughts is, that we shall see our friends again.' JOHNSON. 'Yes, Sir; but you must consider, that when we are become purely rational, many of our friendships will be cut off. Many friendships are formed by a community of sensual pleasures: all these will be cut off. We form many friendships with bad men, because they have agreeable qualities, and they can be useful to us; but, after death, they can no longer be of use to us. We form many friendships by mistake, imagining people to be different from what they really are. After death, we shall see every one in a true light. Then, Sir, they talk of our meeting our relations: but then all relationship is dissolved; and we shall have no regard for one person more than another, but for their real value. However, we shall either have the satisfaction of meeting our friends, or be satisfied without meeting them.' BOSWELL. 'Yet, Sir, we see in scripture, that Dives still retained an anxious concern about his brethren.' JOHNSON. 'Why, Sir, we must either suppose that passage to be metaphorical, or hold with many divines, and all the Purgatorians, that departed souls do not all at once arrive at the utmost perfection of which they are capable.' BOSWELL. 'I think, Sir, that is a very rational supposition.' JOHNSON. 'Why, yes, Sir; but we do not know it is a true one. There is no harm in believing it: but you must not compel others to make it an article of faith; for it is not revealed.' BOSWELL. 'Do you think, Sir, it is wrong in a man who holds the doctrine of Purgatory, to pray for the souls of his deceased friends?' JOHNSON. 'Why no, Sir.' BOSWELL. 'I have been told, that in the Liturgy of the Episcopal Church of Scotland, there was a form of prayer for the dead.' JOHNSON. 'Sir, it is not in the Liturgy which Laud framed for the Episcopal Church of Scotland: if there is a liturgy older than that, I should be glad to see it.' BOSWELL. 'As to our employment in a future state, the sacred writings say little. The Revelation, however, of St. John gives us many ideas, and particularly mentions music.' JOHNSON. 'Why, Sir, ideas must be given you by means of something which you know: and as to music there are some philosophers and divines who have maintained that we shall not be spiritualized to such a degree, but that something of matter, very much refined, will remain. In that case, music may make a part of our future felicity.'

BOSWELL. 'I do not know whether there are any well-attested stories of the appearance of ghosts. You know there is a famous story of the appearance of Mrs. Veal, prefixed to "Drelincourt on Death."' JOHNSON. 'I believe, Sir, that is given up. I believe

the woman declared upon her death-bed that it was a lie.'
BOSWELL. 'This objection is made against the truth of ghosts
appearing: that if they are in a state of happiness, it would be a
punishment to them to return to this world; and if they are in a
state of misery, it would be giving them a respite.' JOHNSON.
'Why, Sir, as the happiness or misery of embodied spirits
does not depend upon place, but is intellectual, we cannot say
that they are less happy or less miserable by appearing upon
earth.'

JAMES BOSWELL, *Life of Samuel Johnson*, year 1772

We begin with this: That the Kingdom of Heaven hath not all
that it must have to a consummate perfection, till it have bodies
too. In those infinite millions of millions of generations, in
which the holy, blessed, and glorious Trinity enjoyed themselves one another, and no more, they thought not their glory so
perfect, but that it might receive an addition from creatures;
and therefore they made a world, a material world, a corporeal
world; they would have bodies. In that noble part of that world
which Moses calls the Firmament, that great expansion from
God's chair to his footstool, from Heaven to earth, there was a
defect, which God did not supply that day, nor the next, but the
fourth day, he did; for that day he made those bodies, those
great and lightsome bodies, the Sun, and Moon, and Stars, and
placed them in the Firmament. So also the Heaven of Heavens,
the Presence Chamber of God himself, expects the presence of
our bodies.

JOHN DONNE (1592–1631), *Sermon*

He was of stature moderately tall, of a straight and equally-
proportioned body, to which all his words and actions gave an
unexpressible addition of comeliness.

The melancholy and pleasant humour were in him so con-
tempered, that each gave advantage to the other, and made his
company one of the delights of mankind.

His fancy was unimitably high, equalled only by his great
wit; both being made useful by a commanding judgement.

His aspect was cheerful, and such as gave a silent testimony of a clear knowing soul, and of a conscience at peace with itself.

His melting eye showed that he had a soft heart, full of noble compassion; of too brave a soul to offer injuries, and too much a Christian not to pardon them in others.

He did much contemplate (especially after he entered into his sacred calling) the mercies of Almighty God, the immortality of the soul, and the joys of heaven; and would often say, in a kind of sacred ecstasy – Blessed be God that he is God, only and divinely like himself.

He was by nature highly passionate, but more apt to reluct at the excesses of it. A great lover of the offices of humanity, and of so merciful a spirit, that he never beheld the miseries of mankind without pity and relief.

He was earnest and unwearied in the search of knowledge; with which his vigorous soul is now satisfied, and employed in a continual praise of that God that first breathed it into his active body: that body, which once was a temple of the Holy Ghost, and is now become a small quantity of Christian dust:

But I shall see it reanimated.

ISAAK WALTON (1593–1683), *Life of Dr John Donne*

Wherever it came from, it has made a sort of spring cleaning in my mind. The dead could be like that; sheer intellects. A Greek philosopher wouldn't have been surprised at an experience like mine. He would have expected that if anything of us remained after death it would be just that. Up to now this always seemed to me a most arid and chilling idea. The absence of emotion repelled me. But in this contact (whether real or apparent) it didn't do anything of the sort. One didn't need emotion. The intimacy was complete – sharply bracing and restorative too – without it. Can that intimacy be love itself – always in this life attended with emotion, not because it is itself an emotion, or needs an attendant emotion, but because our animal souls, our nervous systems, our imaginations, have to respond to it in that way? If so, how many preconceptions I must scrap! A society, a communion, of pure intelligence would not be cold, drab and comfortless. On the other hand it wouldn't be very like what people usually mean when they use such words as 'spiritual', or 'mystical', or 'holy'. It would, if I have had a glimpse, be – well, I'm almost scared at the adjectives I'd have to use. Brisk? cheerful? keen? alert? intense? wide-awake? Above all, solid. Utterly reliable. Firm. There is no nonsense about the dead.

When I say 'intellect' I include will. Attention is an act of will. Intelligence in action is will *par excellence*. What seemed to meet me was full of resolution.

C. S. LEWIS (1898–1963), *A Grief Observed*

'I would by no means dispense with the happiness of believing in a future existence, and, indeed, would say, with Lorenzo de Medici, that those are dead even for this life who hope for no other. But such incomprehensible matters lie too far off to be a theme of daily meditation and thought-distracting speculation. Let him who believes in immortality enjoy his happiness in silence, he has no reason to give himself airs about it. The occasion of Tiedge's "Urania" led me to observe that piety, like nobility, has its aristocracy. I met stupid women, who plumed themselves on believing, with Tiedge, in immortality, and I was forced to bear much dark examination on this point. They were vexed by my saying I should be well pleased if, after the close of this life, we were blessed with another, only I hoped I should hereafter meet none of those who had believed in it here. For how should I be tormented! The pious would throng around me, and say, "Were we not right? Did we not predict it? Has not it happened just as we said?" And so there would be ennui without end even in the other world.

'This occupation with the ideas of immortality,' he continued, 'is for people of rank, and especially ladies, who have nothing to do. But an able man, who has something regular to do here, and must toil and struggle and produce day by day, leaves the future world to itself, and is active and useful in this. Thoughts about immortality are also good for those who have not been very successful here; and I would wager that, if the good Tiedge had enjoyed a better lot, he would also have had better thoughts.'

GOETHE (1749–1832), *Conversations*

Also from E-Alexis Preyre's *The Freedom to Doubt*: 'It is note-worthy that the problem of the soul's immortality becomes less important if one believes in God.'

A *profound* truth. The deeper our experience of earthly light – the closer we get *from here* to the beatific vision – the less we need to rely for our illumination on what Robert Graves once described to me as 'a second helping'. (Not that I wouldn't choose a second helping if offered a choice of that or 'unification with the Godhead' – i.e. a personal obliteration. But only if the next helping involves a further work to be done: *in my present state* eternal bliss has no allure for me at all.)

PHILIP TOYNBEE (1916–81), Part of a Journey

Visited so intensely by so many of the loved-dead. They have been passing *by*, but not in any sense passing *away*, and the message I received (or concocted) was that I would be passing *by* my living friends in the same sort of way. The particular image is of myself at a carriage window, waving to a line of loved ones on the platform as I take a train a few days before they do. And after those few days I shall be on that celestial platform down the line, waiting to greet them one by one; in threes or in dozens as *they* arrive.

(Not to mention the hundreds of beloved dead who arrived long, long before me and were already waiting to greet *me* on my arrival.)

Happy thoughts. And not to be dismissed for that.

PHILIP TOYNBEE, End of a Journey

A life of action and danger moderates the dread of death. It not only gives us fortitude to bear pain, but teaches us at every step the precarious tenure on which we hold our present being. Sedentary and studious men are the most apprehensive on this score. Dr. Johnson was an instance in point. A few years seemed to him soon over, compared with those sweeping contemplations on time and infinity with which he had been used to pose himself. In the *still-life* of a man of letters there was no obvious reason for a change. He might sit in an arm-chair and pour out cups of tea to all eternity. Would it had been possible for him to do so! The most rational cure after all for the inordinate fear of death is to set a just value on life. If we merely wish to continue on the scene to indulge our headstrong humours and tormenting passions, we had better begone at once; and if we only cherish a fondness for existence according to the good we derive from it, the pang we feel at parting with it will not be very severe!

WILLIAM HAZLITT (1778–1830), 'On the Fear of Death'

I am no stranger to deathbeds. To those in pain one talks about themselves; to those of clear mind one praises the world that they are quitting. There is no dignity in leaving a despicable world and the dying are often fearful lest life was not worth the efforts it had cost them. I am never short of subjects to praise.

THORNTON WILDER (1897–1975), *The Ides of March*

'But those who are judged to have lived a life of surpassing holiness – these are they who are released and set free from confinement in these regions of the earth, and passing upward to their pure abode, make their dwelling upon the earth's surface.

'And of these such as have purified themselves sufficiently by philosophy live thereafter altogether without bodies, and reach habitations even more beautiful, which it is not easy to portray – nor is there time to do so now.

'But the reasons which we have already described provide ground enough, as you can see, Simmias, for leaving nothing undone to attain during life some measure of goodness and wisdom; for the prize is glorious and the hope great.

'Of course, no reasonable man ought to insist that the facts are exactly as I have described them. But that either this or something very like it is a true account of our souls and their future habitations – since we have clear evidence that the soul is immortal – this, I think, is both a reasonable contention and a belief worth risking; for the risk is a noble one. We should use such accounts to inspire ourselves with confidence; and that is why I have already drawn out my tale so long.

'There is one way, then, in which a man can be free from all anxiety about the fate of his soul; if in life he has abandoned bodily pleasures and adornments, as foreign to his purpose and likely to do more harm than good, and has devoted himself to the pleasures of acquiring knowledge; and so by decking his soul not with a borrowed beauty but with its own – with self-control, and goodness, and courage, and liberality, and truth – has fitted himself to await his journey to the next world. You, Simmias and Cebes and the rest, will each make this journey some day in the future; but "for me the fated hour" (as a tragic character might say) "calls even now". In other words, it is about time that I took my bath. I prefer to have a bath before drinking the poison, rather than give the women the trouble of washing me when I am dead.'

PLATO, Phaedo, last speech of Socrates

My dear Lady Holland,

I had expected this sad event since Wishaw informed me of the relapse. I received the intelligence of it this morning – frequent enquiries I thought would only give trouble without doing any good. You know me well enough to know that I have the most sincere interest in every important event which befalls Lord Holland and you. The World is full of all sorts of sorrows and miseries – and I think it is better never to have been born – but when evils have happened turn away your mind from them as soon as you can to everything of good which remains. Most people grieve as if grief were a duty or a pleasure, but all who can control it should control it – and remember that these renovations of sorrows are almost the charter and condition under which life is held. God Almighty bless you dear Lady Holland. I would have cut off one of my hands to have saved your little Playfellow – but we must submit. My kindest regards to Lord Holland and Allen.

SYDNEY SMITH (1771–1845), on the death of
Lady Holland's daughter Gina, aged 10

To his wife: all health.

As for the messenger you despatched to tell me of the death of my little daughter, it seems he missed his way as he was going to Athens. But when I came to Tanagra, I heard of it from my niece. I suppose by this time the funeral is over. I wish that whatever has been done may cause you no dissatisfaction, now or hereafter. But if you have purposely left anything undone, waiting for my approval, thinking better to decide it when I am with you, I pray let it be done, without ceremony or timorous superstition, which I know are far from your nature.

Only, dear wife, let us both bear our affliction with patience. I know very well and do comprehend what a loss we have had; but if I should find you grieving beyond measure, this would trouble me more than the thing itself. For I am 'not made of wood or stone', and you know this very well, since I have been your assistant in the education of so many children, whom we brought up at home under our own care. This daughter was born after four sons, when you were longing to bear a daughter, which made me call her by your own name. Therefore I know she was particularly dear to you. And grief must have a special poignancy in one so tenderly affectionate to children, when you call to mind how naturally witty and innocent she was, never angry or fretful. She was naturally mild, and amazingly considerate. And her gratitude and kindness not only gave us delight, but also showed her generous nature: for she would pray her nurse to give suck, not only to other children, but even to her toys, courteously inviting them to her table, as it were, and entertaining them as well as she could.

Now, my dear wife, I see no reason why, when these and other things delighted us so much when she was alive, the remembrance of them should afflict us when she is dead. But I also fear lest, while we cease from sorrowing, we should forget her (as Clymene said, 'I hate the horned bow, and banish youthful pastimes', because she would not be put in mind of her son by the sports he had been used to). For Nature always turns away from things that trouble us. But since our little daughter afforded the sweetest and most charming pleasure to all our senses, so we ought to cherish her memory, which will lead us in many ways – or rather, in many more ways – to joy more than to grief. And it is only right, that the same arguments which we have often used to others should be of help to us at such a time, and that we should not passively sit down and allow the joys which we have tasted to be overwhelmed by a greater mass of new griefs.

PLUTARCH (*c*.50–*c*.125)

Dear Sir,

You have, as I find by every kind of evidence, lost an excellent mother; and I hope you will not think me incapable of partaking of your grief. I have a mother, now eighty-two years of age, whom, therefore, I must soon lose, unless it please God that she should rather mourn for me. I read the letters in which you relate your mother's death to Mrs. Strahan, and think I do myself honour, when I tell you that I read them with tears; but tears are neither to *you* nor to *me* of any farther use, when once the tribute of nature has been paid. The business of life summons us away from useless grief, and calls us to the exercise of those virtues of which we are lamenting our deprivation. The greatest benefit which one friend can confer upon another, is to guard, and excite, and elevate, his virtues. This your mother will still perform, if you diligently preserve the memory of her life, and of her death: a life, so far as I can learn, useful, wise, and innocent; and a death resigned, peaceful, and holy. I cannot forbear to mention, that neither reason nor revelation denies you to hope, that you may increase her happiness by obeying her precepts; and that she may, in her present state, look with pleasure upon every act of virtue to which her instructions or example have contributed. Whether this be more than a pleasing dream, or a just opinion of separate spirits, is, indeed, of no great importance to us, when we consider ourselves as acting under the eye of God: yet, surely, there is something pleasing in the belief, that our separation from those whom we love is merely corporeal; and it may be a great incitement to virtuous friendship, if it can be made probable, that that union that has received the divine approbation shall continue to eternity.

There is one expedient by which you may, in some degree,

continue her presence. If you write down minutely what you remember of her from your earliest years, you will read it with great pleasure, and receive from it many hints of soothing recollection, when time shall remove her yet farther from you, and your grief shall be matured to veneration. To this, however painful for the present, I cannot but advise you, as to a source of comfort and satisfaction in the time to come; for all comfort and all satisfaction is sincerely wished you by, dear Sir,

Your most obliged, most obedient,

And most humble servant,

SAMUEL JOHNSON (1709–84)

Dear Madam,

The grief which I feel for the loss of a very kind friend, is sufficient to make me know how much you suffer by the death of an amiable son: a man, of whom I think it may be truly said, that no one knew him who does not lament him. I look upon myself as having a friend, another friend, taken from me.

Comfort, dear Madam, I would give you, if I could; but I know how little the forms of consolation can avail. Let me, however, counsel you not to waste your health in unprofitable sorrow, but go to Bath, and endeavour to prolong your own life; but when we have all done all that we can, one friend must in time lose the other.

I am, dear Madam,

Your most humble servant,

SAMUEL JOHNSON

Dear Sir,

I am very sorry for your immense loss, which is a repetition of what all feel in this valley of misery and happiness mixed. I send the shadow of the departed angel, and hope the likeness is improved. The lips I have again lessened as you advise, and done a good many other softenings to the whole. I know that our deceased friends are more really with us than when they were apparent to our mortal part. Thirteen years ago I lost a brother, and with his spirit I converse daily and hourly in the spirit, and see him in my remembrance, in the regions of my imagination. I hear his advice, and even now write from his dictate. Forgive me for expressing to you my enthusiasm, which I wish all to partake of, since it is to me a source of immortal joy, even in this world. By it I am the companion of angels. May you continue to be so more and more; and to be more and more persuaded that every mortal loss is an immortal gain. The ruins of Time build mansions in Eternity . . .

WILLIAM BLAKE (1757–1827), to William Hayley on the death of his son

Dear Friend, – Your touching suggestion . . . is a tender permission . . .

We cannot believe for each other – thought is too sacred a despot, but I hope that God, in whatever form, is true to our friend . . . Consciousness is the only home of which we *now* know. That sunny adverb had been enough, were it not fore-closed.

When not inconvenient to your heart, please remember us, and let us help you carry it, if you grow tired. Though we are each unknown to ourself and each other, 'tis not what well conferred it, the dying soldier asks, it is only the water.

> We knew not that we were to live,
> Nor when we are to die
> Our ignorance our cuirass is;
> We wear mortality
> As lightly as an option gown
> Till asked to take it off.
> By His intrusion God is known –
> It is the same with life.

Emily

EMILY DICKINSON (1830–86)

To Sir Robert Cecil, 1597

. . . It is true that you have lost a good and virtuous wife, and myself an honourable friend and kinswoman. But there was a time when she was unknown to you, for whom you then lamented not. She is now no more yours, nor of your acquaintance, but immortal, and not needing of knowing your love or sorrow. Therefore you shall but grieve for that which now is as then it was when not yours, only bettered by the difference in this, that she hath passed the wearisome journey of this dark world, and hath possession of her inheritance.

She hath left behind her the fruit of her love, for whose sake you ought to care for yourself, that you leave them not without a guide, and not by grieving to repine at His will that gave them you, or by sorrowing to dry up your own times that ought to establish them.

I believe it that sorrows are dangerous companions, converting bad into evil and evil into worse, and do no other service than multiply harms. They are the treasures of weak hearts and of the foolish . . .

To Lady Ralegh on the death of their son, 1618
I was loath to write, because I knew not how to comfort you; and God knows, I never knew what sorrow meant till now . . .

SIR WALTER RALEGH (?1554–1618)

About noon that day old Caesar, dead and stiff, was taken by one of the workmen to a green open spot among the old peach trees, where his grave had already been dug. We followed our schoolmaster and watched while the body was lowered and the red earth shovelled in. The grave was deep, and Mr. Trigg assisted in filling it, puffing very much over the task and stopping at intervals to mop his face with his coloured cotton handkerchief.

Then, when all was done, while we were still standing silently around, it came into Mr. Trigg's mind to improve the occasion. Assuming his schoolroom expression he looked round at us and said solemnly: 'That's the end. Every dog has his day and so has every man; and the end is the same for both. We die like old Caesar, and are put into the ground and have the earth shovelled over us.'

Now these simple, common words affected me more than any

other words I have heard in my life. They pierced me to the heart. I had heard something terrible – too terrible to think of, incredible – and yet – and yet if it was not so, why had he said it? Was it because he hated us, just because we were children and he had to teach us our lessons, and wanted to torture us? Alas! no, I could not believe that! Was this, then, the horrible fate that awaited us all? I had heard of death – I knew there was such a thing; I knew that all animals had to die, also that some men died. For how could any one, even a child in its sixth year, overlook such a fact, especially in the country of my birth – a land of battle, murder, and sudden death? I had not forgotten the young man tied to the post in the barn who had killed some one, and would perhaps, I had been told, be killed himself as a punishment. I knew, in fact, that there was good and evil in the world, good and bad men, and the bad men – murderers, thieves, and liars – would all have to die, just like animals; but that there was any life after death I did not know. All the others, myself and my own people included, were good and would never taste death. How it came about that I had got no further in my system or philosophy of life I cannot say; I can only suppose that my mother had not yet begun to give me instruction in such matters on account of my tender years, or else that she had done so and that I had understood it in my own way. Yet, as I discovered later, she was a religious woman, and from infancy I had been taught to kneel and say a little prayer each evening: 'Now I lay me down to sleep, I pray the Lord my soul to keep'; but who the Lord was or what my soul was I had no idea. It was just a pretty little way of saying in rhyme that I was going to bed. My world was a purely material one, and a most wonderful world it was, but how I came to be in it I didn't know; I only knew (or imagined) that I would be in it always, seeing new and strange things every day, and never, never get tired of it. In literature it is only in Vaughan, Traherne, and other mystics, that I find any adequate expression of that perpetual rapturous delight in nature and my own existence which I experienced at that period.

And now these never-to-be-forgotten words spoken over the grave of our old dog had come to awaken me from that beautiful dream of perpetual joy!

When I recall this event I am less astonished at my ignorance than at the intensity of the feeling I experienced, the terrible darkness it brought on so young a mind. The child's mind we think, and in fact know, is like that of the lower animals; or if higher than the animal mind, it is not so high as that of the simplest savage. He cannot concentrate his thought – he cannot think at all; his consciousness is in its dawn; he revels in colours, in odours, is thrilled by touch and taste and sound, and is like a well-nourished pup or kitten at play on a green turf in the sunshine. This being so, one would have thought that the pain of the revelation I had received would have quickly vanished – that the vivid impressions of external things would have blotted it out and restored the harmony. But it was not so; the pain continued and increased until it was no longer to be borne; then I sought my mother, first watching until she was alone in her room. Yet when with her I feared to speak lest with a word she should confirm the dreadful tidings. Looking down, she all at once became alarmed at the sight of my face, and began to question me. Then, struggling against my tears, I told her of the words which had been spoken at the old dog's burial, and asked her if it was true, if I – if she – if all of us had to die and be buried in the ground? She replied that it was not wholly true; it was only true in a way, since our bodies had to die and be buried in the earth, but we had an immortal part which could not die. It was true that old Caesar had been a good, faithful dog, and felt and understood things almost like a human being, and most persons believed that when a dog died he died wholly and had no after-life. We could not know that; some very great, good men had thought differently; they believed that the animals, like us, would live again. That was also her belief – her strong hope; but we could not know for certain, because it had been hidden from us. For ourselves, we knew that we could not really die, because God Himself, who made us and all things, had told us so, and His promise of eternal life had been handed down to us in His Book – in the Bible.

To all this and much more I listened trembling, with a fearful interest, and when I had once grasped the idea that death when it came to me, as it must, would leave me alive after all – that, as she explained, the part of me that really mattered, the myself, the I am I, which knew and considered things, would never perish, I experienced a sudden immense relief. When I went out from her side again I wanted to run and jump for joy.

w. h. hudson (1841–1922), *Far Away and Long Ago*

He who bases or thinks that he bases his conduct – his inward or his outward conduct, his feeling or his action – upon a dogma or theoretical principle which he deems incontrovertible, runs the risk of becoming a fanatic, and moreover, the moment that this dogma is weakened or shattered, the morality based upon it gives way. If the earth that he thought firm begins to rock, he himself trembles at the earthquake, for we do not all come up to the standard of the ideal Stoic who remains undaunted among the ruins of a world shattered into atoms . . .

But he who believes that he is sailing, perhaps without a set course, on an unstable and sinkable raft, must not be dismayed if the raft gives way beneath his feet and threatens to sink. Such a one thinks that he acts, not because he deems his principle of action to be true, but in order to make it true, in order to prove its truth, in order to create his own spiritual world.

miguel de unamuno (1864–1920), *The Tragic Sense of Life*

One thing I become more and more convinced of – that Christians make a terrible error if they base even the slightest part of their faith on any form of survival. Our faith must stand or fall on this that we know – in all its misery, horror, apparent hopelessness. Unless it can make its harsh but saving sense out of what we experience here and now, it is a useless fairy-tale.

Not that we can now *know* there is nothing after death, any more than we can *know* there is something. But even if we knew that we would survive, the faith would still have to depend on *this* reality of matter and spirit for its justification. There is something demeaning and vacuous about the assurance that ultimately we needn't care what happens to us here because all will be wonderfully well afterwards.

Treat death as a blank of ignorance; treat life as something which must be hallowed here and now. Every here: every now.

philip toynbee, *End of a Journey*

Religion in so far as it is a source of consolation is a hindrance to true faith; and in this sense atheism is a purification. I have to be an atheist with that part of myself which is not made for God. Among those in whom the supernatural part of themselves has not been awakened, the atheists are right and the believers wrong . . .

SIMONE WEIL (1909–43), *Notebooks*

When first I was put into prison some people advised me to try and forget who I was. It was ruinous advice. It is only by realising what I am that I have found comfort of any kind. Now I am advised by others to try on my release to forget that I have ever been in a prison at all. I know that would be equally fatal. It would mean that I would be always haunted by an intolerable sense of disgrace, and that those things that are meant as much for me as for anyone else – the beauty of the sun and the moon, the pageant of the seasons, the music of daybreak and the silence of great nights, the rain falling through the leaves, or the dew creeping over the grass and making it silver – would all be tainted for me, and lose their healing power and their power of communicating joy. To reject one's own experiences is to arrest one's own development. To deny one's own experiences is to put a lie into the lips of one's own life. It is no less than a denial of the Soul. For just as the body absorbs things of all kinds, things common and unclean no less than those that the priest or a vision has cleansed, and converts them into swiftness or strength, into the play of beautiful muscles and the moulding of fair flesh, into the curves and colours of the hair, the lips, the eye: so the Soul, in its turn, has its nutritive functions also, and can transform into noble moods of thought, and passions of high import, what in itself is base, cruel, and degrading: nay more, may find in these its most august modes of assertion, and can often reveal itself most perfectly through what was intended to desecrate or destroy.

The fact of my having been the common prisoner of a common gaol I must frankly accept, and, curious as it may seem to you, one of the things I shall have to teach myself is not to be ashamed of it. I must accept it as a punishment, and if one is ashamed of having been punished, one might just as well never have been punished at all. Of course there are many things of which I was convicted that I had not done, but then there are many things of which I was convicted that I had done, and a still greater number of things in my life for which I never was indicted at all. And as for what I have said in this letter, that the gods are strange, and punish us for what is good and humane in us as much as for what is evil and perverse, I must accept the fact that one is punished for the good as well as for the evil that one does. I have no doubt that it is quite right one should be. It helps one, or should help one, to realise both, and not to be too conceited about either. And if I then am not ashamed of my punishment, as I hope not to be, I shall be able to think, and walk, and live with freedom.

OSCAR WILDE (1854–1900), *De Profundis*

My own heart let me more have pity on; let
Me live to my sad self hereafter kind,
Charitable; not live this tormented mind
With this tormented mind tormenting yet.

I cast for comfort I can no more get
By groping round my comfortless, than blind
Eyes in their dark can day or thirst can find
Thirst's all-in-all in all a world of wet.

Soul, self; come, poor Jackself, I do advise
You, jaded, let be; call off thoughts awhile
Elsewhere; leave comfort root-room; let joy size

At God knows when to God knows what; whose smile
's not wrung, see you; unforeseen times rather – as skies
Betweenpie mountains – lights a lovely mile.

GERARD MANLEY HOPKINS (1844–89)

Once in a saintly passion
    I cried with desperate grief,
O Lord, my heart is black with guile,
    Of sinners I am chief.
Then stooped my guardian angel
    And whispered from behind,
'Vanity, my little man,
    You're nothing of the kind.'

JAMES THOMPSON (1834–82)

Were all the world a paradise of ease
    'Twere easy then to live in peace.
Were all men wise, divine, and innocent,
    Just, holy, peaceful, and content,
        Kind, loving, true, and always good,
        As in the Golden Age they stood;
            'Twere easy then to live
In all delight and glory, full of love,
    Blest as the angels are above.

But we such principles must now attain
    (If we true blessedness would gain)
As those are, which will help to make us reign
    Over disorders, injuries,
        Ingratitudes, calamities,
        Affronts, oppressions, slanders, wrongs,
            Lies, angers, bitter tongues;
The reach of malice must surmount, and quell
    The very rage, and power of Hell.

THOMAS TRAHERNE (1637–74), from 'Christian Ethicks'

Use all thy passions – love is thine,
And joy, and jealousy divine;
    Thine hope's eternal fort,
And care thy leisure to disturb,
With fear concupiscence to curb,
    And rapture to transport.

Act simply, as occasion asks;
Put mellow wine in season'd casks;
   Till not with ass and bull:
Remember thy baptismal bond;
Keep from commixtures foul and fond,
   Nor work thy flax with wool.

Distribute: pay the Lord his tithe,
And make the widow's heart-strings blithe;
   Resort with those that weep:
As you from all and each expect,
For all and each thy love direct,
   And render as you reap.

The slander and its bearer spurn,
And propagating praise sojourn
   To make thy welcome last;
Turn from old Adam to the New;
By hope futurity pursue;
   Look upwards to the past.

Control thine eye, salute success,
Honour the wiser, happier bless,
   And for thy neighbour feel;
Grutch not of mammon and his leaven,
Work emulation up to heaven
   By knowledge and by zeal.

O David, highest in the list
Of worthies, on God's ways insist,
   The genuine word repeat.
Vain are the documents of men,
And vain the flourish of the pen
   That keeps the fool's conceit.

Praise above all – for praise prevails;
Heap up the measure, load the scales,
   And good to goodness add:
The generous soul her Saviour aids,
But peevish obloquy degrades;
   The Lord is great and glad.

CHRISTOPHER SMART (1722–71), from *A Song to David*

To look back upon the past year, and see how little we have striven, and to what small purpose; and how often we have been cowardly and hung back, or temerarious and rushed unwisely in; and how every day and all day long we have transgressed the law of kindness; – it may seem a paradox, but in the bitterness of these discoveries a certain consolation resides. Life is not designed to minister to a man's vanity. He goes upon his long business most of the time with a hanging head, and all the time like a blind child. Full of rewards and pleasures as it is – so that to see the day break or the moon rise, or to meet a friend, or to hear the dinner-call when he is hungry, fills him with surprising joys – this world is yet for him no abiding city. Friendships fall through, health fails, weariness assails him; year after year he must thumb the hardly varying record of his own weakness and folly. It is a friendly process of detachment. When the time comes that he should go, there need be few illusions left about himself. *Here lies one who meant well, tried a little, failed much: –* surely that may be his epitaph, of which he need not be ashamed. Nor will he complain at the summons which calls a defeated soldier from the field: defeated, ay, if he were Paul or Marcus Aurelius! – but if there is still one inch of fight in his old spirit, undishonoured. The faith which sustained him in his lifelong blindness and lifelong disappointment will scarce even be required in this last formality of laying down his arms. Give him a march with his old bones; there, out of the glorious sun-coloured earth, out of the day and the dust and the ecstasy – there goes another Faithful Failure!

ROBERT LOUIS STEVENSON (1850–94), A Christmas Sermon

. . . And this was a singular joy and bliss to me that I saw Him *sitting*: for the quiet secureness of sitting showeth endless dwelling.

And He gave me to know truthfully that it was He that showed me all before. And when I had beheld this with heedfulness, then showed our good Lord words, full meekly without voice and without opening of lips, right as He had done before, and said full sweetly: *Know it now well that it was no raving that thou sawest today, but take it and believe it, and keep thee therein, and comfort thee therewith, and trust thou thereto; and thou shalt not be overcome* . . .

And this word, *Thou shalt not be overcome*, was said full clearly and full mightily, for assuredness and comfort against all tribulations that may come. He said not, *Thou shalt not be tempested, thou shalt not be travailed, thou shalt not be afflicted*, but He said, *Thou shalt not be overcome*. God willeth that we take heed to these words, and that we be ever strong in sure trust, in health or in woe. For he loveth and enjoyeth us, and so willeth He that we love and enjoy Him and mightily trust in Him: and *all shall be well*. And soon after all was hidden, and I saw no more.

JULIAN OF NORWICH (*c*.1342–*c*.1416)

When Galileo sent his treatise on the earth's motion to the Grand Duke of Tuscany, he told him that it was meet that that which the higher authorities had determined should be believed and obeyed, and that he considered his treatise 'as poetry or as a dream, and as such I desire your highness to receive it'. And at other times he calls it a 'chimera' or a 'mathematical caprice'. And in the same way in these essays, for fear also – why not confess it? – of the Inquisition, of the modern, the scientific, Inquisition, I offer as a poetry, dream, chimera, mystical caprice, that which springs from what is deepest in me. And I say with Galileo, *Eppur si muove!** But is it only because of this fear? Ah, no! for there is another, more tragic Inquisition, and that is the Inquisition which the modern man, the man of culture, the European – and such am I, whether I will or not – carries within him. There is a more terrible ridicule, and that is the ridicule with which a man contemplates his own self. It is my reason that laughs at my faith and despises it.

MIGUEL DE UNAMUNO, *The Tragic Sense of Life*

* And yet it does move!

I stand for the heart. To the dogs with the head! The reason the mass of men fear God and at bottom dislike Him, is because they rather distrust His heart, and fancy him all brain like a watch.

HERMAN MELVILLE (1819–91), from a letter

                    What is a man
    If his chief good and market of his time
    Be but to sleep and feed? A beast, no more.
    Sure he that made us with such large discourse,
    Looking before and after, gave us not
    That capability and godlike reason
    To fust in us unused . . .

                    WILLIAM SHAKESPEARE (1565–1618), *Hamlet*

God and His profundity. It is possible even for the intelligent man to seek in God that helper and friend whom he can never find. God is the eternal confidant in that tragedy of which each man is hero. Perhaps there are usurers and assassins who say to God: 'Lord, grant that my next enterprise may be successful!' But the prayers of these vile persons do not mar the virtue and joy of my own.

                    CHARLES BAUDELAIRE (1821–67), *Intimate Journals*

I want to cry but God orders me to go on writing. He does not want me to be idle. My wife is crying, crying. I also. I am afraid that the doctor will come and tell me that my wife is crying while I write. I will not go to her, because I am not to blame. My child sees and hears everything and I hope that she will understand me. I love Kyra. My little Kyra feels my love for her, but she thinks too that I am ill, for they have told her so. She asks me whether I sleep well and I tell her that I always sleep well. I do not know what to write, but God wishes me to. Soon I will go to Paris and create a great impression – the whole world will be talking about it. I do not wish people to think that I am a great writer or that I am a great artist nor even that I am a great man. I am a simple man who has suffered a lot. I believe I suffered more than Christ. I love life and want to live, to cry but cannot – I feel such a pain in my soul – a pain which frightens me. My soul is ill. My soul, not my mind. The doctors do not understand my illness. I know what I need to get well. My illness is too great to be cured quickly. I am incurable. My soul is ill, I am poor, a pauper, miserable. Everyone who reads these lines will suffer – they will understand my feelings. I know what I need. I am strong, not weak. My body is not ill – it is my soul that is ill. I suffer, I suffer. Everyone will feel and understand, I am a man, not a beast. I love everyone, I have faults, I am a man – not God. I want to be God and therefore I try to improve myself. I want to dance, to draw, to play the piano, to write verses, I want to love everybody. That is the object of my life. I know that Socialists would understand me better – but I am not a Socialist. I am a part of God, my party is God's party. I love everybody. I *do not* want war or frontiers. The world exists. I have a home everywhere. I live everywhere. I do not want to have any property. I do not want to be rich. I want to love. I am love – not cruelty. I am not a bloodthirsty animal. I am man. I am man. God is in me. I am in God. I want Him, I seek Him. I want my manuscripts to be published so that everybody can read them. I hope to improve myself. I do not know how to, but I feel that God will help all those who seek Him. I am a seeker, for I can feel God. God seeks me and therefore we will find each other.

> God and Nijinsky,
> *Saint Moritz-Dorf,*
> *Villa Guardamunt,*
> *February 27th,* 1919

VASLAV NIJINSKY (1890–1950), *Diary*

And slowly answered Arthur from the barge:
'The old order changeth, yielding place to new,
And God fulfils Himself in many ways,
Lest one good custom should corrupt the world.
Comfort thyself: what comfort is in me?
I have lived my life, and that which I have done
May He within Himself make pure! but thou,
If thou shouldst never see my face again,
Pray for my soul. More things are wrought by prayer
Than this world dreams of.'

ALFRED TENNYSON (1809–92), *Morte d'Arthur*

I must create a System or be enslaved by another man's.
I will not reason and compare: my business is to create.

WILLIAM BLAKE, *Jerusalem*

How can one joy absorb another? are not different joys Holy,
Eternal, Infinite? and each joy is a Love.

WILLIAM BLAKE, *Visions of the Daughters of Albion*

The representation of Hermes in a state of erection, with its
mysterious significance, of which Herodotus (of Pelasgian
origin) speaks, has doubtless the same meaning as the one
contained in those words of Ramakrishna: 'Just as a flighty
woman, as she goes about her household duties, is perpetually
thinking of the rendezvous she has with her lover – so in the
same way, whatever you may be doing, never cease for a
moment to think of God' . . .

Freud's doctrine would be absolutely true if the conception
behind it were not oriented in such a manner as to make it
absolutely false.

To reproach mystics with loving God by means of the faculty
of sexual love is as though one were to reproach a painter with
making pictures by means of colours composed of material
substances. We haven't anything else with which to love. One
might just as well, moreover, address the same reproach to
a man who loves a woman. The whole of Freudian doctrine
is saturated with the very prejudice which he makes it his
mission to combat, namely, that everything that is sexual is
base.

SIMONE WEIL, *Notebooks*

And I do think that man is related to the universe in some
'religious' way, even prior to his relation to his fellow man. And
I do think that the only way of true relationship between men is
to meet in some common 'belief' – if the belief is but physical
and not merely mental. I hate religion in its religiosity as much
as you do. But you, who like etymologies, look at religion.

Monism is the religion of the cut-off, father-worship is the cult of the cut-off: but it's the cut-offness that's to fault. There is a *principle* in the universe, towards which man turns religiously – a *life* of the universe itself. And the hero is he who touches and transmits the life of the universe.

D. H. LAWRENCE (1885–1930), from a letter

For I have learned
To look on nature, not as in the hour
Of thoughtless youth; but hearing oftentimes
The still, sad music of humanity,
Nor harsh nor grating, though of ample power
To chasten and subdue. And I have felt
A presence that disturbs me with the joy
Of elevated thoughts; a sense sublime
Of something far more deeply interfused,
Whose dwelling is the light of setting suns,
And the round ocean and the living air,
And the blue sky, and in the mind of man;
A motion and a spirit, that impels
All thinking things, all objects of all thought,
And rolls through all things. Therefore am I still
A lover of the meadows and the woods,
And mountains; and of all that we behold
From this green earth; of all the mighty world
Of eye, and ear, – both what they half create,
And what perceive; well pleased to recognise
In nature and the language of the sense,
The anchor of my purest thoughts, the nurse,
The guide, the guardian of my heart, and soul
Of all my moral being . . .

WILLIAM WORDSWORTH (1770–1850), from 'Tintern Abbey'

One day I was walking over a bit of marshy ground close to Inchy Wood when I felt, all of a sudden, and only for a second, an emotion which I said to myself was the root of Christian mysticism. There had swept over me a sense of weakness, of

dependence on a great personal Being somewhere far off yet
near at hand. No thought of mine had prepared me for this
emotion, for I had been preoccupied with Aengus and Edain,
and with Manannan, Son of the Sea. That night I awoke lying
upon my back and hearing a voice speaking above me and
saying, 'No human soul is like any other human soul, and
therefore the love of God for any human soul is infinite, for no
other soul can satisfy the same need in God.'

W. B. YEATS (1865–1939), *Mythologies*

. . . And they conversed together in visionary forms dramatic
   which bright
Redounded from their tongues in thunderous majesty, in
   visions
In new expanses, creating exemplars of Memory and of
   Intellect,
Creating Space, creating Time, according to the wonders
   divine
Of Human Imagination throughout all the three regions
   immense
Of childhood, manhood, and old age; and the all-
   tremendous unfathomable Non-ens
Of death was seen in regenerations terrific or complacent,
   varying
According to the subject of discourse; and every word and
   every character
Was human . . .

WILLIAM BLAKE, *Jerusalem*

Chanting the square deific, out of the One advancing, out of
   the sides;
Out of the old and new – out of the square entirely divine,
Solid, four-sided, (all the sides needed), from this side
   JEHOVAH am I,
Old Brahm I, and I Saturnius am;
Not Time affects me – I am Time, modern as any;
Unpersuadable, relentless, executing righteous judgments;

As the Earth, the Father, the brown old Kronos, with laws,
Aged beyond computation – yet ever new – ever with those
    mighty laws rolling,
Relentless, I forgive no man – whoever sins, dies – I will
    have that man's life;
Therefore let none expect mercy – have the seasons,
    gravitation, the appointed days, mercy? – no more have I;
But as the seasons, and gravitation – and as all the
    appointed days, that forgive not,
I dispense from this side judgments inexorable, without the
    least remorse.

Consolator most mild, the promised one advancing,
With gentle hand extended, the mightier God am I,
Foretold by prophets and poets, in their most rapt
    prophecies and poems;
From this side, lo! the Lord CHRIST gazes – lo! Hermes I – lo!
    mine is Hercules' face;
All sorrow, labor, suffering, I, tallying it, absorb in myself;
Many times have I been rejected, taunted, put in prison, and
    crucified – and many times shall be again;
All the world have I given up for my dear brothers' and
    sisters' sake – for the soul's sake;
Wending my way through the homes of men, rich or poor,
    with the kiss of affection;
For I am affection – I am the cheer-bringing God, with hope,
    and all-enclosing charity;
(Conqueror yet – for before me all the armies and soldiers of
    the earth shall yet bow – and all the weapons of war
    become impotent);
With indulgent words, as to children – with fresh and sane
    words, mine only;
Young and strong I pass, knowing well I am destined myself
    to an early death:
But my charity has no death – my wisdom dies not, neither
    early nor late,
And my sweet love, bequeathed here and elsewhere, never
    dies.

Aloof, dissatisfied, plotting revolt,
Comrade of criminals, brother of slaves,
Crafty, despised, a drudge, ignorant,
With sudra face and worn brow – black, but in the depths of
    my heart, proud as any;
Lifted, now and always, against whoever, scorning, assumes
    to rule me;
Morose, full of guile, full of reminiscences, brooding, with
    many wiles,
(Though it was thought I was baffled and dispelled, and my
    wiles done – but that will never be);
Defiant, I, SATAN, still live – still utter words – in new lands
    duly appearing, (and old ones also);
Permanent here, from my side, warlike, equal with any, real
    as any,
Nor time, nor change, shall ever change me or my words.

SANTA SPIRITA, breather, life,
Beyond the light, lighter than light,
Beyond the flames of hell – joyous, leaping easily above hell;
Beyond Paradise – perfumed solely with mine own perfume;
Including all life on earth – touching, including God –
    including Saviour and Satan;
Ethereal, pervading all, (for without me, what were all? what
    were God?)
Essence of forms – life of the real identities, permanent,
    positive, (namely the unseen),
Life of the great round world, the sun and stars, and of man
    – I, the general Soul,
Here the square finishing, the solid, I the most solid,
Breathe my breath also through these little songs.

        WALT WHITMAN (1819–92), 'Chanting the Square Deific'

    And now what are we? unbelievers both,
    Calm and complete, determinately fixed
    To-day, to-morrow, and for ever, pray?
    You'll guarantee me that? Not so, I think.
    In no-wise! all we've gained is, that belief,

As unbelief before, shakes us by fits,
Confounds us like its predecessor. Where's
The gain? how can we guard our unbelief,
Make it bear fruit to us? – the problem here.
Just when we are safest, there's a sunset-touch,
A fancy from a flower-bell, someone's death,
A chorus-ending from Euripides –
And that's enough for fifty hopes and fears
As old and new at once as Nature's self,
To rap and knock and enter in our soul,
Take hands and dance there, a fantastic ring,
Round the ancient idol, on his base again –
The grand Perhaps! We look on helplessly –
There the old misgivings, crooked questions are –
This good God – what he could do, if he would,
Would, if he could – then must have done long since:
If so, when, where, and how? some way must be –
Once feel about, and soon or late you hit
Some sense, in which it might be, after all.
Why not, 'The Way, the Truth, the Life?'

                                        – That way

Over the mountain, which who stands upon
Is apt to doubt if it's indeed a road;
While if he views it from the waste itself,
Up goes the line there, plain from base to brow,
Not vague, mistakeable! what's a break or two
Seen from the unbroken desert either side?
And then (to bring in fresh philosophy)
What if the breaks themselves should prove at last
The most consummate of contrivances
To train a man's eye, teach him what is faith, –
And so we stumble at truth's very test?
What have we gained then by our unbelief
But a life of doubt diversified by faith,
For one of faith diversified by doubt.
We called the chess-board white, – we call it black.

ROBERT BROWNING (1812–89),
from 'Bishop Blougram's Apology'

. . . But that also, with its assured belief in heaven and hell as two countries in which to live, has gone, and now we do, both in word and in deed, believe in the continuous life of the world of men, and as it were, add every day of that common life to the little stock of days which our own mere individual experience wins for us: and consequently we are happy. Do you wonder at it? In times past, indeed, men were told to love their kind, to believe in the religion of humanity and so forth. But look you, just in the degree that a man had elevation of mind and refinement enough to be able to value this idea, was he repelled by the obvious aspect of the individuals composing the mass which he was to worship; and he could only evade that repulsion by making a conventional abstraction of mankind that had little actual or historical relation to the race; which to his eyes was divided into blind tyrants on the one hand and apathetic degraded slaves on the other.

But now, where is the difficulty in accepting the religion of humanity, when the men and women who go to make up humanity are free, happy, and energetic at least, and most commonly beautiful of body also, and surrounded by beautiful things of their own fashioning, and a nature bettered and not worsened by contact with mankind? This is what this age of the world has reserved for us.

WILLIAM MORRIS (1834–96), News from Nowhere

Because the gods are vanishing, because it is now no longer possible to believe that earthly affairs are subject to an arbitrary supernatural interference, it by no means follows that religion is dead. The deepest religious mood is a religious mood that in no way depends upon belief in a God. The highest form of faith is a Godless faith. We have pretended long enough. We must allow our spirits to sink like stones to the bottom of the pond. Mud is a more honest and dependable substance than is air or water. The true religion is the religion of the atheist. By day and by night men and women who belong to this ancient foundation cast themselves as low as the very grass in passionate worship. They are sustained by no sense of benevolent wardship. No eye sees them, no ear hears them. There is none to shepherd their wayfaring, yet their outcast spirits never cease from acclaiming what is. Merely to be alive, to be abroad upon the earth, is justification enough.

LLEWELYN POWYS (1884–1939), *Glory of Life*

Go thy way, eat thy bread with joy, and drink thy wine with a merry heart; for God hath already accepted thy works. Let thy garments be always white; and let not thy head lack ointment. Live joyfully with the wife whom thou lovest all the days of the life of thy vanity, which he hath given thee under the sun, all the days of thy vanity: for that is thy portion in life, and in thy labour wherein thou labourest under the sun. Whatsoever thy hand findeth to do, do it with thy might; for there is no work, nor device, nor knowledge, nor wisdom, in the grave, whither thou goest.

Ecclesiastes (late 3rd century BC)

. . . I only know that many of these exceptional moments brought with them a peculiar horror and a physical collapse; they seemed dominant; myself passive. This suggests that as one gets older one has a greater power through reason to provide an explanation; and that this explanation blunts the sledge-hammer force of the blow. I think this is true, because though I still have the peculiarity that I receive these sudden shocks, they are now always welcome; after the first surprise, I always feel instantly that they are particularly valuable.

And so I go on to suppose that the shock-receiving capacity is what makes me a writer. I hazard the explanation that a shock is at once in my case followed by the desire to explain it. I feel that I have had a blow; but it is not, as I thought as a child, simply a blow from an enemy hidden behind the cotton wool of daily life; it is or will become a revelation of some order; it is a token of some real thing behind appearances; and I make it real by putting it into words. It is only by putting it into words that I make it whole; this wholeness means that it has lost its power to hurt me; it gives me, perhaps because by doing so I take away the pain, a great delight to put the severed parts together.

Perhaps this is the strongest pleasure known to me. It is the rapture I get when in writing I seem to be discovering what belongs to what; making a scene come right; making a character come together. From this I reach what I might call a philosophy; at any rate it is a constant idea of mine; that behind the cotton wool is hidden a pattern; that we – I mean all human beings – are connected with this; that the whole world is a work of art; that we are parts of the work of art. *Hamlet* or a Beethoven quartet is the truth about this vast mass that we call the world. But there is no Shakespeare, there is no Beethoven; certainly and emphatically there is no God; we are the words; we are the music; we are the thing itself. And I see this when I have a shock.

VIRGINIA WOOLF (1882–1941), Moments of Being

Not to believe in the immortality of the soul, but to look upon the whole of life as destined to prepare for the moment of death; not to believe in God, but to love the universe, always, even in the throes of anguish, as a home – there lies the road toward faith by way of atheism . . .

SIMONE WEIL, Notebooks

. . . The production and birth of this superior personality is what is meant when our text speaks of the 'holy fruit', the 'diamond body', or any other kind of incorruptible body. Psychologically, these expressions symbolize an attitude that is beyond the reach of emotional entanglements and violent shocks – a consciousness detached from the world. I have reasons for believing that this attitude sets in after middle life and is a natural preparation for death. Death is psychologically as important as birth and, like it, is an integral part of life. What happens to the detached consciousness in the end is a question the psychologist cannot be expected to answer. Whatever his theoretical position he would hopelessly overstep the bounds of his scientific competence. He can only point out that the views of our text in regard to the timelessness of the detached consciousness are in harmony with the religious thought of all ages and with that of the overwhelming majority of mankind. Anyone who thought differently would be standing outside the human order and would, therefore, be suffering from a disturbed psychic equilibrium. As a doctor, I make every effort to strengthen the belief in immortality, especially with older patients when such questions come threateningly close. For, seen in correct psychological perspective, death is not an end but a goal, and life's inclination towards death begins as soon as the meridian is passed.

CARL JUNG (1875–1961), *Alchemical Studies*

Mock on, Mock on, Voltaire, Rousseau;
Mock on, Mock on; 'tis all in vain!
You throw the sand against the wind,
And the wind blows it back again.

And every sand becomes a Gem
Reflected in the beams divine;
Blown back they blind the mocking eye,
But still in Israel's path they shine.

The Atoms of Democritus
And Newton's Particles of light
Are sands upon the Red Sea shore,
Where Israel's tents do shine so bright.

WILLIAM BLAKE

DEFIANCE

Blake defies the eighteenth-century rationalists in his own way. Emerson seems to defy Time itself; Patmore shrugs, defiantly. The transcendent is put to the back of the mind (of those in which it was ever present), and life is faced without it. Henry Miller turns a man at the bottom of the social heap nearly into an ikon; Tom o' Bedlam sings the song of the outcast, and Falstaff dismisses the fine abstractions of society altogether. Clare, Thoreau, Henley, Gay show self against the world in an extreme form.

Edgar Allan Poe laments with unspoken defiance. Omar Khayyam forgives God, preferring that to being forgiven. Byron raises an eyebrow coolly, leaving the door slightly ajar; and Arnold, who feels that the door is shut, turns back to the room and its only other occupant.

This is a mood, only crudely called 'defiance', which leads here to a subtler form of it, which could be called 'comedy', a final sense of the uselessness of all our fundamental questions.

The debt is paid,
The verdict said,
The Furies laid,
The plague is stayed,
All fortunes made;
Turn the key and bolt the door,
Sweet is death for evermore.
Nor haughty hope, nor swart chagrin,
Nor murdering hate, can enter in.
All is now secure and fast;
Not the gods can shake the Past;
Flies-to the adamantine door
Bolted down forevermore.
None can re-enter there –
No thief so politic,
No Satan with a royal trick
Steal in by window, chink, or hole,
To bind or unbind, add what lacked,
Insert a leaf, or forge a name,
New-face or finish what is packed,
Alter or mend eternal Fact.

RALPH WALDO EMERSON (1803–82), 'The Past

Here, in this little Bay,
Full of tumultuous life and great repose,
Where, twice a day,
The purposeless, glad ocean comes and goes,
Under high cliffs, and far from the huge town,
I sit me down.
For want of me the world's course will not fail:
When all its work is done, the lie shall rot;

> The truth is great, and shall prevail,
> When none cares whether it prevail or not.
>
> COVENTRY PATMORE (1823–96), '*Magna est Veritas*'

> Now all the truth is out,
> Be secret and take defeat
> From any brazen throat,
> For how can you compete,
> Being honour bred, with one
> Who, were it proved he lies,
> Were neither shamed in his own
> Nor in his neighbours' eyes?
> Bred to a harder thing
> Than Triumph, turn away
> And like a laughing string
> Whereon mad fingers play
> Amid a place of stone,
> Be secret and exult,
> Because of all things known
> That is most difficult.
>
> W. B. YEATS (1865–1939), 'To a Friend Whose
Work Has Come to Nothing'

Ah poverties, wincings, and sulky retreats,
Ah you foes that in conflict have overcome me,
(For what is my life or any man's life but a conflict with foes,
    the old, the incessant war?)
You degradations, you tussle with passions and
    appetites,
You smarts from dissatisfied friendships (ah wounds the
    sharpest of all!)
You toil of painful and choked articulations, you
    meannesses,
You shallow tongue-talks at tables (my tongue the
    shallowest of any);
You broken resolutions, you racking angers, you
    smothered ennuis!

Ah think not you finally triumph, my real self has yet to
    come forth,
It shall yet march forth o'ermastering, till all lies beneath
    me,
It shall yet stand up the soldier of ultimate victory.

WALT WHITMAN (1819–92), Leaves of Grass

Fall, leaves, fall; die, flowers, away;
Lengthen night and shorten day;
Every leaf speaks bliss to me
Fluttering from the autumn tree.
I shall smile when wreaths of snow
Blossom where the rose should grow;
I shall sing when night's decay
Ushers in a drearier day.

EMILY BRONTË (1818–48)

I do not know what I may appear to the world; but to myself I
seem to have been only like a boy, playing on the sea-shore, and
diverting myself, in now and then finding a smoother pebble or
prettier shell than ordinary, while the great ocean of truth lay
all undiscovered before me.

SIR ISAAC NEWTON (1642–1727), Memoirs

Towards the end of the meal each evening the *veilleur de nuit*
drops in for his bit of cheer. This is the only human being in the
whole institution with whom I feel a kinship. He is a nobody.
He carries a lantern and a bunch of keys. He makes the rounds
through the night, stiff as an automaton. About the time the
stale cheese is being passed around, in he pops for his glass of
wine. He stands there, with paw outstretched, his hair stiff and
wiry, like a mastiff's, his cheeks ruddy, his mustache gleaming
with snow. He mumbles a word or two and Quasimodo brings
him the bottle. Then, with feet solidly planted, he throws back
his head and down it goes, slowly in one long draught. To me
it's like he's pouring rubies down his gullet. Something about

this gesture which seizes me by the hair. It's almost as if he were drinking down the dregs of human sympathy, as if all the love and compassion in the world could be tossed off like that, in one gulp – as if that were all that could be squeezed together day after day. A little less than a rabbit they have made him. In the scheme of things he's not worth the brine to pickle a herring. He's just a piece of live manure. And he knows it. When he looks around after his drink and smiles at us, the world seems to be falling to pieces. It's a smile thrown across an abyss. The whole stinking civilized world lies like a quagmire at the bottom of the pit, and over it, like a mirage, hovers this wavering smile.

HENRY MILLER (1891–1980), *Tropic of Cancer*

From the hag and hungry goblin
That into rags would rend ye,
And the spirit that stands by the naked man
In the Book of Moons defend ye!
That of your five sound senses
You never be forsaken,
Nor wander from yourselves with Tom
Abroad to beg your bacon.

While I do sing 'any food, any feeding,
Feeding, drink or clothing',
Come dame or maid, be not afraid,
Poor Tom will injure nothing . . .

With a host of furious fancies,
Whereof I am commander,
With a burning spear, and a horse of air,
To the wilderness I wander.
By a knight of ghosts and shadows
I summoned am to tourney,
Ten leagues beyond the wide world's end:
Methink it is no journey.

ANON. (16th–17th century), 'Tom o' Bedlam's Song'

FALSTAFF: I would 'twere bed-time, Hal, and all well.

PRINCE HENRY: Why, thou owest God a death.

FALSTAFF: 'Tis not due yet, I would be loath to pay him before his day – what need I be so forward with him that calls not on me? Well, 'tis no matter, honour pricks me on. Yea, but how if honour prick me off when I come on, how then? Can honour set to a leg? No. Or an arm? No. Or take away the grief of a wound? No. Honour hath no skill in surgery then? No. What is honour? A word. What is in that word honour? What is that honour? Air. A trim reckoning! Who hath it? He that died a-Wednesday. Doth he feel it? No. Doth he hear it? No. 'Tis insensible, then? Yea, to the dead. But will it not live with the living? No. Why? Detraction will not suffer it. Therefore I'll none of it. Honour is a mere scutcheon – and so ends my catechism.

WILLIAM SHAKESPEARE (1564–1616), *Henry IV, Part I*

I am: yet what I am none cares or knows
　　My friends forsake me like a memory lost,
I am the self-consumer of my woes –
　　They rise and vanish in oblivious host,
Like shadows in love's frenzied stifled throes: –
And yet I am, and live – like vapours tost

Into the nothingness of scorn and noise,
　　Into the living sea of waking dreams,
Where there is neither sense of life or joys,
　　But the vast shipwreck of my life's esteems;
Even the dearest, that I love the best,
Are strange – nay, rather stranger than the rest.

I long for scenes, where man hath never trod,
　　A place where woman never smiled or wept –
There to abide with my Creator, God,
　　And sleep as I in childhood sweetly slept,
Untroubling, and untroubled where I lie,
The grass below – above the vaulted sky.

JOHN CLARE (1793–1864)

They made me erect and lone
And within me is the bone
Where I sit there is my throne.
If ye choose to sit apart
If ye choose give me the start
Take the sap and leave the heart.
Still my vision will be clear
Still my life will not be drear:
To the center all is near.

HENRY DAVID THOREAU (1817–62)

Out of the night that covers me,
 Black as the pit from pole to pole,
I thank whatever gods may be
 For my unconquerable soul.

In the fell clutch of circumstance
 I have not winced nor cried aloud:
Under the bludgeonings of chance
 My head is bloody, but unbowed.

Beyond this place of wrath and tears
 Looms but the Horror of the shade,
And yet the menace of the years
 Finds and shall find me unafraid.

It matters not how strait the gate,
 How charged with punishments the scroll,
I am the master of my fate:
 I am the captain of my soul.

W. E. HENLEY (1849–1903), *'Invictus'*

Life is a jest, and all things show it;
I thought so once, but now I know it.

JOHN GAY (1685–1732), 'My Own Epitaph'

> . . . How ever, fare you well:
> Though in our miseries Fortune have a part,
> Yet in our noble sufferings she hath none –
> Contempt of pain, that we may call our own.
>
> JOHN WEBSTER (*c.*1578–*c.*1632), *Duchess of Malfi*

I met a traveller from an antique land
Who said: 'Two vast and trunkless legs of stone
Stand in the desert . . . Near them, on the sand,
Half sunk, a shattered visage lies, whose frown,
And wrinkled lip, and sneer of cold command,
Tell that its sculptor well those passions read
Which yet survive, stamped on these lifeless things,
The hand that mocked them, and the heart that fed;
And on the pedestal these words appear:
"My name is Ozymandias, king of kings:
Look on my works, ye Mighty, and despair!"
Nothing beside remains. Round the decay
Of that colossal wreck, boundless and bare
The lone and level sands stretch far away.'

P. B. SHELLEY (1792–1822), 'Ozymandias'

Take this kiss upon the brow!
And, in parting from you now,
Thus much let me avow –
You are not wrong, who deem
That my days have been a dream;
Yet if hope has flown away
In a night, or in a day,
In a vision, or in none,
Is it therefore the less *gone?*
All that we see or seem
Is but a dream within a dream.

I stand amid the roar
Of a surf-tormented shore,
And I hold within my hand

Grains of the golden sand –
How few! yet how they creep
Through my fingers to the deep,
While I weep – while I weep!
O God! can I not grasp
Them with a tighter clasp?
O God! can I not save
One from the pitiless wave?
Is *all* that we see or seem
But a dream within a dream?

EDGAR ALLAN POE (1809–49)

What! out of senseless Nothing to provoke
A conscious Something to resent the yoke
    Of unpermitted Pleasure, under pain
Of Everlasting Penalties, if broke!

What! from his helpless Creature be repaid
Pure Gold for what he lent him dross-allayed –
    Sue for a Debt we never did contract,
And cannot answer – Oh, the sorry trade!

Oh Thou, who didst with pitfall and with gin
Beset the Road I was to wander in,
    Thou wilt not with Predestined Evil round
Enmesh, and then impute my Fall to Sin!

Oh Thou, who Man of baser Earth didst make
And even with Paradise devise the Snake:
    For all the Sin wherewith the Face of Man
Is blackened – Man's Forgiveness give – and take!

EDWARD FITZGERALD (1809–93),
from *The Rubaiyat of Omar Khayyam*

I have not loved the world, nor the world me;
I have not flattered its rank breath, nor bowed
To its idolatries a patient knee,
Nor coined my cheek to smiles, nor cried aloud
In worship of an echo; in the crowd
They could not deem me one of such; I stood
Among them, but not of them; in a shroud
Of thoughts which were not their thoughts, and still could,
Had I not filed my mind, which thus itself subdued.

I have not loved the world, nor the world me –
But let us part fair foes; I do believe,
Though I have found them not, that there may be
Words which are things, hopes which will not deceive,
And virtues which are merciful, nor weave
Snares for the failing; I would also deem
O'er others' grief that some sincerely grieve;
That two, or one, are almost what they seem,
That goodness is no name, and happiness no dream.

LORD BYRON (1788–1824), from Childe Harold's Pilgrimage

The sea is calm to-night.
The tide is full, the moon lies fair
Upon the straits; on the French coast, the light
Gleams, and is gone; the cliffs of England stand,
Glimmering and vast, out in the tranquil bay.
Come to the window, sweet is the night-air!
Only, from the lone line of spray
Where the sea meets the moon-blanched sand,
Listen! you hear the grating roar
Of pebbles which the waves draw back, and fling,
At their return, up the high strand,
Begin, and cease, and then again begin,
With tremulous cadence slow, and bring
The eternal note of sadness in.

Sophocles long ago
Heard it on the Ægæan, and it brought

Into his mind the turbid ebb and flow
Of human misery; we
Find also in the sound a thought,
Hearing it by this distant northern sea.

The Sea of Faith
Was once, too, at the full, and round earth's shore
Lay like the folds of a bright girdle furled.
But now I only hear
Its melancholy, long, withdrawing roar,
Retreating, to the breath
Of the night-wind down the vast edges drear
And naked shingles of the world.

Ah, love, let us be true
To one another! for the world, which seems
To lie before us like a land of dreams,
So various, so beautiful, so new,
Hath really neither joy, nor love, nor light,
Nor certitude, nor peace, nor help for pain;
And we are here as on a darkling plain
Swept with confused alarms of struggle and flight,
Where ignorant armies clash by night.

MATTHEW ARNOLD (1822–88), 'Dover Beach'

COMEDY

Comedy in the widest sense, for how else could it begin with Job, and include Marcus Aurelius? The word 'comedy' stretched as far as when those of Shakespeare's plays which are not tragedies or histories are given that name. Nevertheless a useful category because, a refinement of defiance, it is the acknowledgement of the uselessness of self-interrogation. It is not necessarily an evasion.

Job hears a fierce God talking (but not answering). C. S. Lewis imagines a divine headmaster. Marcus Aurelius doubts the propriety of pestering the gods, it is a form of bad manners. Garrison Keillor puts this in a contemporary way and Lewis Carroll disguises and versifies it, ending on those two terminal points of useless, circular discussion, 'but . . .' and 'Goodbye'. Robert Graves takes this point of view out of sight.

The refusal of people to discuss these questions over dinner disappoints Boswell; Whitman agrees with Johnson's answer, and Jane Austen suggests a method of dealing with disappointment. Cyril Connolly has other methods, and Ivor Gurney his own.

Montaigne's revelations about his character contain the comedy that all such honesty must. We recognize something of ourselves in his description and perhaps also in Yeats's of his hypochondriac uncle, to whom gloom was a consolation.

The possession of money can be a consolation (solace, distraction, but consolation also): this is admitted, ironically, by Clough; its superficiality underlined by Praed. Byron presents a list of consolations, money-derived, and Swift a list of the consolations some can derive from the failing of another's health – in this case, his own.

Oh if only God would hear me,
 state his case against me,
 let me read his indictment.
I would carry it on my shoulder
 or wear it on my head like a crown.
I would justify the least of my actions;
 I would stand before him like a prince . . .

THEN THE UNNAMEABLE ANSWERED JOB
FROM WITHIN THE WHIRLWIND:

Who is this whose ignorant words
 smear my design with darkness?
Stand up now like a man;
 I will question you: please, instruct me.

Where were you when I planned the earth?
 Tell me, if you are so wise.
Do you know who took its dimensions,
 measuring its length with a cord?
What were its pillars built on?
 Who laid down its cornerstone,
while the morning stars burst out singing
 and the angels shouted for joy!

Were you there when I stopped the waters,
 as they issued gushing from the womb?
when I wrapped the ocean in clouds
 and swaddled the sea in shadows?
when I closed it in with barriers
 and set its boundaries, saying,
'Here you may come, but no farther;
 here shall your proud waves break'? . . .

The Book of Job (c.450 BC)

When I lay these questions before God I get no answer. But a rather special sort of 'No answer'. It is not the locked door. It is more like a silent, certainly not uncompassionate, gaze. As though He shook His head not in refusal but waiving the question. Like, 'Peace, child; you don't understand.'

Can a mortal ask questions which God finds unanswerable? Quite easily, I should think. All nonsense questions are unanswerable. How many hours are there in a mile? Is yellow square or round? Probably half the questions we ask – half our great theological and metaphysical problems – are like that.

C. S. LEWIS (1898–1963), *A Grief Observed*

Can the gods, who have contrived all else so well and so benevolently, have overlooked this one thing, that even eminently virtuous men, men in the closest correspondence with the divine and living in intimate union with it through their good works and devotion, should know no re-birth after their death, but be doomed to utter extinction? However, should this indeed be their lot, rest assured that if there had been need for some different plan, it would have been so ordained; had it accorded with Nature, Nature would have brought it to pass. Therefore, from its not being so (if in truth it is not), you may have all confidence that it ought not to be so. Surely you can see that in raising idle questions like this you are indicting the deity? For should we even be joining issue with the gods in this way, unless they were supremely good and just? And if they are, how could they ever have permitted anything to be unfairly or unreasonably neglected in their dispositions for the universe?

MARCUS AURELIUS (121–180), *Meditations*

Between the tree line and my left elbow, a billion stars in the sky, each representing a billion we couldn't see. We lay in the grass, thinking about America and also a little bit about snakes and about spiders clambering from blade to blade who might rappel down into our mouths, and looked open-mouthed up at the heavens, and everything we said out loud seemed hilarious to us. Tiny us gazing up at the South Wall of the Unimaginable

Everything and feeling an obligation to comment, and our most profound comments sounded like peas dropped in a big empty bucket. 'It makes you feel small, doesn't it.' *Plink.* 'I used to know the names of those.' *Plunk.* One more peabrain having to share the effect that the world is having on him. 'It's beautiful, isn't it . . . I remember when I was a kid –' someone said and we laughed ourselves limp – Shut up, we said, laughing, we're sick of sensitive people, everything you see just reminds you of yourself! So stick it in your ear.

GARRISON KEILLOR (b.1942), We Are Still Married

'As to poetry, you know,' said Humpty Dumpty, stretching out one of his great hands, '*I* can repeat poetry as well as other folk, if it comes to that—'

'Oh, it needn't come to that!' Alice hastily said, hoping to keep him from beginning.

'The piece I'm going to repeat,' he went on without noticing her remark, 'was written entirely for your amusement.'

Alice felt that in that case she really *ought* to listen to it; so she sat down, and said 'Thank you' rather sadly.

> *'In winter, when the fields are white,*
> *I sing this song for your delight—*

only I don't sing it,' he added, as an explanation.

'I see you don't,' said Alice.

'If you can *see* whether I'm singing or not, you've sharper eyes than most,' Humpty Dumpty remarked severely. Alice was silent.

> *'In spring, when woods are getting green,*
> *I'll try and tell you what I mean:'*

'Thank you very much,' said Alice.

> *'In summer, when the days are long,*
> *Perhaps you'll understand the song:*
>
> *In autumn, when the leaves are brown,*
> *Take pen and ink, and write it down.'*

'I will, if I can remember it so long,' said Alice.

'You needn't go on making remarks like that,' Humpty Dumpty said: 'they're not sensible, and they put me out.'

> *'I sent a message to the fish:*
> *I told them "This is what I wish."*
>
> *The little fishes of the sea,*
> *They sent an answer back to me.*
>
> *The little fishes' answer was*
> *"We cannot do it, Sir, because—"'*

'I'm afraid I don't quite understand,' said Alice.

'It gets easier further on,' Humpty Dumpty replied.

> *'I sent to them again to say*
> *"It will be better to obey."*
>
> *The fishes answered, with a grin,*
> *"Why, what a temper you are in!"*
>
> *I told them once, I told them twice:*
> *They would not listen to advice.*
>
> *I took a kettle large and new,*
> *Fit for the deed I had to do.*
>
> *My heart went hop, my heart went thump:*
> *I filled the kettle at the pump.*
>
> *Then some one came to me and said*
> *"The little fishes are in bed."*
>
> *I said to him, I said it plain,*
> *"Then you must wake them up again."*
>
> *I said it very loud and clear:*
> *I went and shouted in his ear.'*

Humpty Dumpty raised his voice almost to a scream as he repeated this verse, and Alice thought, with a shudder, 'I wouldn't have been the messenger for *anything*!'

> *'But he was very stiff and proud:*
> *He said "You needn't shout so loud!"*

And he was very proud and stiff:
He said "I'd go and wake them, if—"

I took a corkscrew from the shelf:
I went to wake them up myself.

And when I found the door was locked,
I pulled and pushed and kicked and knocked.

And when I found the door was shut,
I tried to turn the handle, but—'

There was a long pause.
'Is that all?' Alice timidly asked.
'That's all,' said Humpty Dumpty. 'Good-bye.'

LEWIS CARROLL (1832–98), Through the Looking-Glass

MR FLOSKY: This rage for novelty is the bane of literature. Except my works and those of my particular friends, nothing is good that is not as old as Jeremy Taylor: and, *entre nous*, the best parts of my friends' books were either written or suggested by myself.

THE HONOURABLE MR LISTLESS: Sir, I reverence you. But I must say, modern books are very consolatory and congenial to my feelings. There is, as it were, a delightful north-east wind, an intellectual blight breathing through them; a delicious misanthropy and discontent, that demonstrates the nullity of virtue and energy, and puts me in good humour with myself and my sofa.

MR FLOSKY: Very true, sir. Modern literature is a north-east wind – a blight of the human soul. I take credit to myself for having made it so. The way to produce fine fruit is to blight the flower. Marry, so be it. Ponder thereon.

THOMAS LOVE PEACOCK (1785–1866), Nightmare Abbey

The Bellman perceived that their spirits were low,
    And repeated in musical tone
Some jokes he had kept for a season of woe –
    But the crew would do nothing but groan.

LEWIS CARROLL, The Hunting of the Snark

'But that was nothing to what things came out
From the sea-caves of Criccieth yonder.'
'What were they? Mermaids? dragons? ghosts?'
'Nothing at all of any things like that.'
'What were they, then?'
                   'All sorts of queer things,
Things never seen or heard or written about,
Very strange, un-Welsh, utterly peculiar
Things. Oh, solid enough they seemed to touch,
Had anyone dared it. Marvellous creation,
All various shapes and sizes, and no sizes,
All new, each perfectly unlike his neighbour,
Though all came moving slowly out together.'
'Describe just one of them.'
                      'I am unable.'
'What were their colours?'
                   'Mostly nameless colours,
Colours you'd like to see; but one was puce
Or perhaps more like crimson, but not purplish.
Some had no colour.'
                'Tell me, had they legs?'
'Not a leg nor foot among them that I saw.'
'But did these things come out in any order?
What o'clock was it? What was the day of the week?
Who else was present? How was the weather?'
'I was coming to that. It was half-past three
On Easter Tuesday last. The sun was shining.
The Harlech Silver Band played *Marchog Jesu*
On thirty-seven shimmering instruments,
Collecting for Carnarvon's (Fever) Hospital Fund.
The populations of Pwllheli, Criccieth,
Portmadoc, Borth, Tremadoc, Penrhyndeudraeth,

Were all assembled. Criccieth's mayor addressed them
First in good Welsh and then in fluent English,
Twisting his fingers in his chain of office,
Welcoming the things. They came out on the sand,
Not keeping time to the band, moving seaward
Silently at a snail's pace. But at last
The most odd, indescribable thing of all,
Which hardly one man there could see for wonder
Did something recognizably a something.'
'Well, what?'
              'It made a noise.'
                           'A frightening noise?'
'No, no.'
       'A musical noise? A noise of scuffling?'
'No, but a very loud, respectable noise –
Like groaning to oneself on Sunday morning
In Chapel, close before the second psalm.'
'What did the mayor do?'
                     'I was coming to that.'

        ROBERT GRAVES (1895–1985), 'Welsh Incident'

When I complained of having dined at a splendid table without
hearing one sentence of conversation worthy of being remembered, he said, 'Sir, there seldom is any such conversation.'
BOSWELL. 'Why then meet at table?' JOHNSON. 'Why to eat and
drink together, and to promote kindness; and, Sir, this is better
done when there is no solid conversation: for when there is,
people differ in opinion, and get into bad humour, or some of
the company who are not capable of such conversation, are left
out, and feel themselves uneasy. It was for this reason Sir
Robert Walpole said, he always talked bawdy at his table,
because in that all could join.'

        JAMES BOSWELL, *Life of Samuel Johnson*, year 1777

I have perceived that to be with those I like is enough,
To stop in company with the rest at evening is enough,
To be surrounded by beautiful, curious, breathing, laughing
　flesh is enough,
To pass among them or touch any one, or rest my arm ever
　so lightly round his or her neck for a moment, what is this
　then?
I do not ask any more delight, I swim in it as in a sea.
There is something in staying close to men and women and
　looking on them, and in the contact and odor of them, that
　pleases the soul well,
All things please the soul, but these please the soul well.

WALT WHITMAN (1819–92), from 'I Sing the Body Electric'

Upon the whole, therefore, she found, what has been sometimes found before, that an event to which she had looked
forward with impatient desire did not, in taking place, bring all
the satisfaction she had promised herself. It was consequently
necessary to name some other period for the commencement of
actual felicity – to have some other point on which her wishes
and hopes might be fixed, and by again enjoying the pleasure of
anticipation, console herself for the present, and prepare for
another disappointment. Her tour to the Lakes was now the
object of her happiest thoughts; it was her best consolation for
all the uncomfortable hours which the discontentedness of her
mother and Kitty made inevitable; and could she have included Jane in the scheme, every part of it would have been
perfect.

'But it is fortunate,' thought she, 'that I have something to
wish for. Were the whole arrangement complete, my disappointment would be certain. But here, by carrying with me one
ceaseless source of regret in my sister's absence, I may reasonably hope to have all my expectations of pleasure realized. A
scheme of which every part promises delight can never be
successful; and general disappointment is only warded off by
the defence of some little peculiar vexation.'

JANE AUSTEN (1775–1817), *Pride and Prejudice*

Causes of Angst: Angst is inherent in the uncoiling of the ego, the *ver solitaire*. It dwells in the *Lacrimæ Rerum*, in the contrasting of the Past with the Present. It lurks in old loves, in old letters and in our despair at the complexity of modern life.

Effect: Misery, disgust, tears, guilt.

Temporary cures: (1) Lunch with a new friend, gossip, literary talk, i.e. appeals to vanity; (2) Art (Renoir landscapes), the true escape into *Timelessness*; (3) The office personality (Alibi Ike); (4) Old friends, relationships dating from before the Fall.

CYRIL CONNOLLY (1903–74), *The Unquiet Grave*

Had I a song
I would sing it here
Four lined square shaped
Utterance dear

But since I have none,
Well, regret in verse
Before the power's gone
Might be worse, might be worse.

IVOR GURNEY (1890–1937)

I have never had a taste for any sort of tiresome labour. I have hardly ever managed any business but my own; or if I have, it has been on condition that I did things in my own time and in my own way. And I have only acted for people who trusted me, and did not bother me, and knew me well. For expert riders will get some service even from a restive and broken-winded horse.

Even my childish upbringing was gentle and free, and subject to no rigorous discipline. All this bred in me a sensitive disposition, incapable of bearing worries; to such a degree that I like to have any losses or troubles that concern me concealed from my knowledge. I enter under the head of expenses the sum that it costs me to keep my negligence fed and maintained.

MONTAIGNE (1533–92), 'On Presumption'

The memory is an instrument of wonderful utility, and without it the judgement can hardly perform its duties; I am almost completely without it. Anything that is put before me must be presented piecemeal. For it is beyond my powers to reply to a proposition with several heads. I cannot take a message if I have not put it down in my notebook; and when I have an important speech to make that is of any length, I am reduced to the mean and miserable necessity of learning by heart, word for word, what I am going to say. Otherwise, I should have neither power nor assurance, but should always be afraid that my memory was going to play me a trick. But this method is just as difficult for me. It takes me three hours to learn three lines; and then, if I have composed it myself, the freedom and authority with which I change the order, or alter a word, and my constant variations of matter, make it more difficult to keep in mind. Now, the more I distrust my memory, the more confused it becomes; it serves me best by accident, I have to woo it unconcernedly. For if I press it, it becomes bewildered; and once it has begun to waver, the more I sound it the more perplexed and embarrassed it grows; it serves me at its own hours, not at mine.

This same defect that I find in my memory, I find also in several other places. I avoid commands, obligations, and constraint. What I do easily and naturally, I can no longer do if I command myself to do it by an express and definite injunction. In the case of my body too, those organs that have some liberty and special jurisdiction over themselves at times refuse to obey me, when I fix and bind them to a particular place and hour for the service I need of them. This compulsive and tyrannical prescription offends them; either from fear or spite, they shrink and grow numb.

Once, long ago, I was in a place where it is considered a barbarous discourtesy not to respond to those who pledge you a toast; and, though I was allowed complete freedom, I tried to be convivial, according to the custom of the country, in order to please the ladies of the party. But there was an amusing result. For this threat, and my preparations forcibly to make myself violate my natural habits, so choked my throat that I could not swallow a single drop, and I was unable to drink even the amount I needed for my meal. I found myself full, and my thirst was quenched by the quantity of drink that I had consumed in my thoughts.

This defect is most apparent in those who have the strongest and most active imaginations; yet it is natural, and there is no one who does not feel it in some degree. An excellent archer, who had been condemned to death, was offered his life if he would give some noteworthy proof of his skill. But he refused to try, fearing that the excessive strain on his will might cause him to miss his aim, and that far from saving his life, he would also forfeit the reputation he had acquired as a marksman. A man whose thoughts are elsewhere will not fail to take the same number and length of steps almost to an inch, every time that he walks in a particular place. But if he applies his attention to measuring and counting them, he will find that what he did naturally and by chance, he will not do as accurately by design.

My library, which is a fine one for a country library, is situated at one corner of my house. But if anything occurs to me that I want to look up or write down there, I have to entrust it to some other person for fear that it will escape me merely as I cross my courtyard. If I venture in speaking to wander ever so little from my argument, I never fail to lose it; which is the reason why I keep myself short, concise, and terse in my conversation. I am obliged to call the men who serve me by the names of their offices or their provinces, for I find it very hard to remember a name. I can tell, to be sure, that it has three syllables, that it sounds harsh, and that it begins or ends with a certain letter. And, if I live long enough, I am not sure that I shall not forget my own name, as others have done.

MONTAIGNE, 'On Presumption'

George Pollexfen was as patient as his father was impetuous, and did all by habit. A well-to-do, elderly man, he lived with no more comfort than when he had set out as a young man. He had a little house and one old general servant and a man to look after his horse, and every year he gave up some activity and found that there was one more food that disagreed with him. A hypochondriac, he passed from winter to summer through a series of woollens that had always to be weighed; for in April or May, or whatever the date was, he had to be sure he carried the exact number of ounces he had carried upon that date since boyhood. He lived in despondency, finding in the most cheerful news reasons of discouragement, and sighing every twenty-second of June over the shortening of the days. Once in later years, when I met him in Dublin sweating in a mid-summer noon, I brought him into the hall of the Kildare Street Library, a cool and shady place, without lightening his spirits; for he but said in a melancholy voice, 'How very cold this place must be in winter-time.' Sometimes when I had pitted my cheerfulness against his gloom over the breakfast-table, maintaining that neither his talent nor his memory nor his health were running to the dregs, he would rout me with the sentence, 'How very old I shall be in twenty years.'

W. B. YEATS (1865–1939), *Autobiographies*

Thus I sat at my table *en grand seigneur*,
And when I had done threw a crust to the poor;
Not only the pleasure, one's self, of good eating,
But also the pleasure of now and then treating.
   So pleasant it is to have money, heigh ho!
   So pleasant it is to have money.

They may talk as they please about what they call pelf,
And how one ought never to think of one's self,
And how pleasures of thought surpass eating and drinking –
My pleasure of thought is the pleasure of thinking
   How pleasant it is to have money, heigh ho!
   How pleasant it is to have money.

ARTHUR HUGH CLOUGH (1819–61), from 'Dipsychus'

   Good-night to the Season! another
     Will come with its trifles and toys,
   And hurry away, like its brother,
     In sunshine, and odour, and noise.
   Will it come with a rose, or a brier?
     Will it come with a blessing, or curse?

Will its bonnets be lower, or higher?
    Will its morals be better, or worse?
Will it find me grown thinner, or fatter,
    Or fonder of wrong or of right,
Or married, or buried? – no matter, –
    Good-night to the Season! – Good-night!

WINTHROP MACKWORTH PRAED (1802–39),
from 'The Season'

. . . The fair sex should be always fair; and no man
Till thirty, should perceive there's a plain woman.

And after that serene and somewhat dull
    Epoch, that awkward corner turned for days
More quiet, when our moon's no more at full,
    We may presume to criticise or praise;
Because indifference begins to lull
    Our passions, and we walk in wisdom's ways;
Also because the figure and the face
Hint, that 'tis time to give the younger place.

I know that some would fain postpone this era,
    Reluctant as all placemen to resign
Their post; but theirs is merely a chimera,
    For they have pass'd life's equinoctial line:
But then they have their claret and Madeira
    To irrigate the dryness of decline;
And county meetings, and the parliament,
And debt, and what not, for their solace sent.

And is there not religion, and reform,
    Peace, war, the taxes, and what's called the 'Nation'?
The struggle to be pilots in a storm?
    The landed and the monied speculation?
The joys of mutual hate to keep them warm
    Instead of love, that mere hallucination?
Now hatred is by far the longest pleasure;
Men love in haste, but they detest at leisure.

LORD BYRON (1788–1824), *Don Juan*

The time is not remote, when I
Must by the course of nature die;
When I foresee my special friends
Will try to find their private ends,
Though it is hardly understood
Which way my death can do them good;
Yet thus, methinks, I hear 'em speak:
'See, how the Dean begins to break:
Poor gentleman, he droops apace,
You plainly find it in his face;
That old vertigo in his head
Will never leave him, till he's dead.
Besides, his memory decays,
He recollects not what he says;
He cannot call his friends to mind,
Forgets the place where last he dined;
Plies you with stories o'er and o'er:
He told them fifty times before.
How does he fancy we can sit
To hear his out-of-fashioned wit?
But he takes up with younger folks,
Who for his wine will bear his jokes:
Faith, he must make his stories shorter,
Or change his comrades once a quarter;
In half the time, he talks them round;
There must another set be found.

   'For poetry, he's past his prime,
He takes an hour to find a rhyme:
His fire is out, his wit decayed,
His fancy sunk, his Muse a jade.
I'd have him throw away his pen;
But there's no talking to some men.'

   And then their tenderness appears,
By adding largely to my years:
'He's older than he would be reckoned,
And well remembers Charles the Second.

   'He hardly drinks a pint of wine,
And that, I doubt, is no good sign.
His stomach too begins to fail:

Last year we thought him strong and hale;
But now he's quite another thing,
I wish he may hold out till spring.'
   Then hug themselves, and reason thus:
'It is not yet so bad with us.' . . .

JONATHAN SWIFT (1667–1745),
from 'Verses on the Death of Dr Swift'

PLEASURES

Pleasures or enjoyments: keeping as closely as possible to their consolatory nature. However, Blake, in his pleasures of the imagination, puts his finger on a difficulty, one touched on by Bellow earlier, and by others: why some of us remain *in*consolable, so that even our own happiness, and that of others, is insufficient to alleviate a sense of the unhappiness of the world. 'The tree,' says Blake, 'which moves some to tears of joy, is in the eyes of others only a green thing which stands in the way.' (Perhaps it would have been more accurate for him to say that most of us can be both those kinds of people, at different times.) To Traherne, also, it is a mystery 'that the world is both a paradise and a prison to different persons'. His counsel is that we should avoid the latter kind, the 'prisoners', for our own peace of mind, which is good advice, but the puzzle will not go away. It is as though there are two basic temperaments, both with their justification: those capable of being happy, in certain circumstances, and those, given the same chance, for whom the circumstances are not right. It is possible that this latter kind of nature finds its consolation in social and political action, in other words in *changing* the circumstances. These natures do not believe, as Marcus Aurelius did, that man's soul is 'his most untroubled retreat'. It will have become clear already that the consolations gathered here are Marcus-Aurelian, a species of internal reorganization, a basis for action rather than action itself. External activity, and the consolation of social and political results arising from it, would make a different book – perhaps a slimmer one.

Coleridge, temporarily imprisoned in his lime-tree bower (some boiling water had spilled on to his foot), presents the archetype of the man bent on internal reorganization, on making the best of things. His imagination has been fired by the natural scenes outside his house, and he imagines his friends enthusing on the walk in the Quantocks which he had intended to take with them. One of those friends was Charles Lamb, and perhaps he was not so fired as Coleridge hoped; as Lamb explains to Wordsworth in a letter filled with the pleasures of the town.

Yet, for us, the difficulty of the two temperaments, one capable of being consoled, the other not quite, still nags. Elizabeth Browning suggests this, and Whitman in the face of the problem surrenders himself to what sounds like a vital form of sleep. Fletcher celebrates, gratefully, the pleasure of the real thing.

Marvell, Grigson, Connolly, Neruda *enjoy*, with different degrees of simplicity. There follow various pleasures of the flesh – drink, sex, food (and sleep, again). Shakespeare's Duke in the forest finds 'good in everything', though he has a scruple about hunting. Byron obliquely acknowledges this scruple – 'Tis no sport for peasants' – and sings the pleasures of the English autumn which do not include hunting.

Nature, as a source of imaginative and sensual pleasure, has been celebrated. Now comes a more particular response to it: Clare's minute observation; a scientist's sudden tenderness for it (Humphrey Davy), nature as an affect rather than a substitute religion. This leads to an (on the whole) unanthropomorphic pleasure in animals: Cowper's hare, and the unabashed, pleasant sentimentality of William Watson's epitaph for his dog, undercut by Edward Thomas's exasperated recognition of a bird-killing cat's right to exist. Nature can give us hints of some possible transcendence (Dufault) partly because it is never precisely the same; and, by keeping a close eye on it, Gurney suggests we can make it our own in defiance of Time.

This 'keeping an eye' brings us to art, the pleasure it gives and the pleasure artists take in making it. Keats finds that poetry makes everything of interest. Patrick Kavanagh gives a new generation of Irish poets liberty to write about what they know. Ruskin celebrates this liberty in Giotto; and Leopardi gives the widest possible reach to art's liberty to console.

The artist consoled by his own sense of creativity is evident in Pasternak. To Arnold and Yeats poetry is a form of faith; Herbert's faith leads to it. Forster (with his arranged table) and Keats ('adonizing') give us pictures of writers getting down to work. It is consoling to learn that they need such homely tricks. William Byrd on the usefulness of learning to sing; Browning on the usefulness of composers.

Fun I love, but too much Fun is of all things the most loathsome. Mirth is better than Fun, and Happiness is better than Mirth. I feel that a man may be happy in this world. And I know that this world is a world of Imagination and Vision. I see every thing I paint in this world, but every body does not see alike. To the eyes of a miser a guinea is far more beautiful than the sun, and a bag worn with the use of money has more beautiful proportions than a vine filled with grapes. The tree which moves some to tears of joy is in the eyes of others only a green thing which stands in the way. Some see Nature all ridicule and deformity, and by these I shall not regulate my proportions; and some scarce see Nature at all. But to the eyes of the man of imagination, Nature is Imagination itself. As a man is, so he sees. As the eye is formed, such are its powers. You certainly mistake, when you say that the visions of Fancy are not to be found in this world. To me this world is all one continued vision of Fancy or Imagination, and I feel flattered when I am told so. What is it sets Homer, Virgil, and Milton in so high a rank of art? Why is the Bible more entertaining and instructive than any other book? Is it not because they are addressed to the imagination, which is spiritual sensation, and but mediately to the understanding or reason?

WILLIAM BLAKE (1757–1827), from a letter

For the Poison which they drank hath infatuated their fancies and now they know not, neither will they understand, they walk on in darkness. *All the foundations of the Earth are out of course.* It is safety not to be with them. And a great part of happiness to be freed from their seducing and enslaving errors. That while others live in a Golgotha or prison, we should be in Eden, is a very great mystery. And a mercy it is that we should be rejoicing in the temple of Heaven, while they are toiling and lamenting in Hell, for the world is both a paradise and a prison to different persons.

THOMAS TRAHERNE (1637–74)

Now, my friends emerge
Beneath the wide wide Heaven – and view again
The many-steepled tract magnificent
Of hilly fields and meadows, and the sea,
With some fair bark, perhaps, whose sails light up
The slip of smooth clear blue betwixt two Isles
Of purple shadow! Yes! they wander on
In gladness all; but thou, methinks, most glad,
My gentle-hearted Charles! for thou hast pined
And hungered after Nature, many a year,
In the great City pent, winning thy way
With sad yet patient soul, through evil and pain
And strange calamity! Ah! slowly sink
Behind the western ridge, thou glorious Sun!
Shine in the slant beams of the sinking orb,
Ye purple heath-flowers! richlier burn, ye clouds!
Live in the yellow light, ye distant groves!
And kindle, thou blue Ocean! So my friend
Struck with deep joy, may stand, as I have stood,
Silent with swimming sense; yea, gazing round
On the wide landscape, gaze till all doth seem
Less gross than bodily, and of such hues
As veil the Almighty Spirit, when yet he makes
Spirits perceive his presence.
A delight
Comes sudden on my heart, and I am glad
As I myself were there! Nor in this bower,
This little lime-tree bower, have I not marked
Much that has soothed me. Pale beneath the blaze
Hung the transparent foliage; and I watched
Some broad and sunny leaf, and loved to see
The shadow of the leaf and stem above
Dappling its sunshine! And that walnut-tree

Was richly tinged, and a deep radiance lay
Full on the ancient ivy, which usurps
Those fronting elms, and now, with blackest mass
Makes their dark branches gleam a lighter hue
Through the late twilight: and though now the bat
Wheels silent by, and not a swallow twitters,
Yet still the solitary humble-bee
Sings in the bean-flower! Henceforth I shall know
That Nature ne'er deserts the wise and pure;
No plot so narrow, be but Nature there,
No waste so vacant, but may well employ
Each faculty of sense, and keep the heart
Awake to Love and Beauty! and sometimes
'Tis well to be bereft of promised good,
That we may lift the soul, and contemplate
With lively joy the joys we cannot share.
My gentle-hearted Charles! when the last rook
Beat its straight path along the dusky air
Homewards, I blest it! deeming its black wing
(Now a dim speck, now vanishing in light)
Had crossed the mighty Orb's dilated glory,
While thou stood'st gazing; or, when all was still,
Flew creeking o'er thy head, and had a charm
For thee, my gentle-hearted Charles, to whom
No sound is dissonant which tells of Life.

s. t. coleridge (1772–1834),
from 'This Lime-Tree Bower My Prison', 1797

I ought before this to have replied to your very kind invitation into Cumberland. With you and your sister I could gang any where. But I am afraid whether I shall ever be able to afford so desperate a Journey. Separate from the pleasure of your company, I dont much care if I never see a mountain in my life. I have passed all my days in London, until I have formed as many and intense local attachments, as any of your mountaineers can have done with dead nature. The lighted shops of the Strand and Fleet Street, the innumerable trades, treadesmen and customers, coaches, waggons, playhouses, all the bustle and wickedness round about Covent Garden, the very women of the Town, the watchmen, drunken scenes, rattles, – life awake, if you awake, at all hours of the night, the impossibility of being dull in Fleet Street, the crowds, the very dirt and mud, the Sun shining upon houses and pavements, the print shops, the old book stalls, parsons cheapening books, coffee houses, steams of soups from kitchens, the pantomimes, London itself a pantomime and a masquerade, – all these things work themselves into my mind and feed me without a power of satiating me. The wonder of these sights impells me into nightwalks about the crowded streets, and I often shed tears in the motley Strand from fulness of joy at so much Life. – All these emotions must be strange to you. So are your rural emotions to me. But consider, what must I have been doing all my life, not to have lent great portions of my heart with usury to such scenes?

My attachments are all local, purely local. I have no passion (or have had none since I was in love, and then it was the spurious engendering of poetry and books) to groves and vallies. The rooms where I was born, the furniture which has been before my eyes all my life, a book case which has followed me about (like a faithful dog, only exceeding him in knowledge) wherever I have moved, old tables, streets, squares, where I have sunned myself, my old school – these are my mistresses. Have I not enough, without your mountains? I do not envy you. I should pity you, did I not know, that the Mind will make friends of any thing. Your sun and moon and skies and hills and lakes affect me no more, or scarcely come to me in more venerable characters, than as a gilded room with tapestry and tapers, where I might live with handsome visible objects. I consider the clouds above me but as a roof, beautifully painted, but unable to satisfy the mind, and at last, like the pictures of the apartment of a connoisseur, unable to afford him any longer a pleasure. So fading upon me, from disuse, have been the Beauties of Nature, as they have been confinedly called; so ever fresh and green and warm are all the inventions of men in this great city.

CHARLES LAMB (1775–1834), from a letter to Wordsworth

Men seek for seclusion in the wilderness, by the seashore, or in the mountains – a dream you have cherished only too fondly yourself. But such fancies are wholly unworthy of a philosopher, since at any moment you choose you can retire within yourself. Nowhere can man find a quieter or more untroubled retreat than in his own soul; above all, he who possesses resources in himself, which he need only contemplate to secure immediate ease of mind – the ease that is but another word for a well-ordered spirit. Avail yourself often, then, of this retirement, and so continually renew yourself.

MARCUS AURELIUS (121–180)

What's the best thing in the world?
June-rose, by May-dew impearled;
Sweet south-wind, that means no rain;
Truth, not cruel to a friend;
Pleasure, not in haste to end;
Beauty, not self-decked and curled
Till its pride is over-plain;
Light, that never makes you wink;
Memory, that gives no pain;
Love, when, *so*, you're loved again.
What's the best thing in the world?
– Something out of it, I think.

ELIZABETH BARRETT BROWNING (1806–61),
'The Best Thing in the World'

This is thy hour O Soul, thy free flight into the wordless,
Away from books, away from art, the day erased, the lesson done,
Thee fully forth emerging, silent, gazing, pondering the themes thou lovest best,
Night, sleep, death and the stars.

WALT WHITMAN (1819–92), 'A Clear Midnight'

Care-charming Sleep, thou easer of all woes,
Brother to Death, sweetly thyself dispose
On this afflicted prince, fall like a cloud
In gentle showers; give nothing that is loud
Or painful to his slumbers; easy, sweet,
And as a purling stream, thou son of Night,
Pass by his troubled senses; sing his pain
Like hollow murmuring wind, or silver rain;
Into this prince gently, oh gently slide,
And kiss him into slumbers like a bride.

JOHN FLETCHER (1579–1625), *The Tragedy of Valentinian*

What wondrous life is this I lead!
Ripe apples drop about my head;
The luscious clusters of the vine
Upon my mouth do crush their wine;
The nectarine, and curious peach,
Into my hands themselves do reach;
Stumbling on melons, as I pass,
Ensnared with flowers, I fall on grass.

Meanwhile the mind, from pleasures less,
Withdraws into its happiness:
The mind, that ocean where each kind
Does straight its own resemblance find,
Yet it creates, transcending these,
Far other worlds, and other seas,
Annihilating all that's made
To a green thought in a green shade.

ANDREW MARVELL (1621–78), from 'The Garden'

Why – I find I am always asking this kind of question, and
leaving it unanswered, or incompletely answered – why do I so
much enjoy finding one of these neolithic polishing or sharpen-
ing stones, and – if necessary – pushing the muck out of its
grooves, uncovering a polished furrow, a made-by-man furrow,
continuing smooth with his energy?

I don't have to think of the people who squatted on these boulders pushing and pulling axes of honey flint forwards and backwards, and coating them again with a little sand and water. If I did I would have to think of the axemakers as savage, without tenderness, given to head-hunting, to shaping brain-balls, to cannibalism.

I think of them – I suppose – in a blurred way as peoplers of space (this grey emptiness so unlike anything in England) and of time so much before my time. I comfort myself when I feel along one of these silky-surfaced grooves worn across and into the rough naturalness of the stone. I don't – in *polissoirs*, in dolmens, in Iron Age camps – make communion with the dead, except vaguely: I don't touch a work of art: I make a lair for myself.

GEOFFREY GRIGSON (1905–85), *Notes from an Odd Country*

Like the glow-worm; dowdy, minute, passive, yet full of mystery to the poet and erotic significance to its fellows; so everything and everybody eternally radiate a dim light for those who care to seek. The strawberry hidden under the last leaf cries, 'Pick me'; the forgotten book, in the forgotten bookshop, screams to be discovered. The old house hidden in the hollow agitates itself violently at the approach of its pre-destined admirer. Dead authors cry 'Read me'; dead friends say 'Remember me'; dead ancestors whisper, 'Unearth me'; dead places, 'Revisit me'; and sympathetic spirits, living and dead, are continually trying to enter into communion. Physical or intellectual attraction between two people is a constant communication. Underneath the rational and voluntary world lies the involuntary, impulsive, integrated world, the world of Relation in which everything is one; where sympathy and antipathy are engrossed in their selective tug-of-war.

We learn a new word for the first time. Then it turns up within the next hour. Why? Because words are living organisms impelled by a crystallizing process to mysterious agglutinative matings at which the word-fancier is sometimes privileged to assist. The glow-worms light up . . . The individual also is like a moving mirror or screen which reflects in its motion an ever-changing panorama of thoughts, sensations, faces and places, and yet the screen is always being guided to reflect one film rather than another, always seeking a chosen *querencia*. In the warm sea of experience we blob around like plankton, we love-absorb or hate-avoid each other or are avoided or are absorbed, devoured and devouring. Yet we are no more free than the cells in a plant or the microbes in a drop of water but are all held firmly in tension by the pull of the future and the tug of the past.

CYRIL CONNOLLY (1903–74), *The Unquiet Grave*

At last, a day with no need to think, no need to fill it, a day that can give itself orders, as days should: with no human inter-ference, woven smoothly, day-coloured, smelling of shade, of sky, of its own latitude.

Once I used to collect these blue-winged days, hoarded them closely, classified them (summer days, dark days, dawns), but they escaped from their cages, continued life on their own . . . Days with no gummed paper, no decisions, no aspirins; physi-cally pure as mineral traces . . .

PABLO NERUDA (1904–73)

After the long suicidal winter Pleasure comes to rescue us from the desert island of the ego and allow us two months' grace. Good-bye sick Pascal and his mouldy troupe; gaunt Kierkegaard, hunch-backed Leopardi, wheezing Proust and limping Epictetus with his Open Door! Midsummer greeting to La Fontaine, Congreve, Aristippus, Horace and Voltaire! Good-bye morning tears, 'All-is-lost', never-again, doubt, des-pair! Welcome cheese-breathing hang-over, tipsy mornings for gargling poetry, asparagus afternoons, gull's-egg evenings, affection slopping over into gossip, who-was-there and ring-a-ling! Taoism at last rewarded! 'Flower o' the Quince', . . . Hour of the Broad Bean.

If all the world loved pleasure as much as Palinurus there would be no war.

CYRIL CONNOLLY, *The Unquiet Grave*

Had I my wish, I would distend my guts
  As wide as from the north to southern skies,
And have at once as many mouths and throats
  As old Briareus arms, or Argos eyes.
The raging sea's unpalatable brine,
  That drowns so many thousands in a year,
I'd turn into an ocean of good wine,
  And for my cup would choose the hemisphere;
Would then perform the wager Xanthus laid,
  In spite of all the river's flowing streams,
Swill till I pissed a deluge, then to bed,
  And please my thirsty soul with small-beer dreams.

EDWARD WARD (1667–1731),
'The Extravagant Drunkard's Wish'

In our way, Johnson strongly expressed his love of driving fast in a post-chaise. 'If (said he) I had no duties, and no reference to futurity, I would spend my life in driving briskly in a post-chaise with a pretty woman; but she should be one who could understand me, and would add something to the conversation.'

JAMES BOSWELL, *Life of Samuel Johnson*, year 1777

> *Green grow the rashes, O;*
> *Green grow the rashes, O;*
> *The sweetest hours that e'er I spent,*
> *Are spent amang the lasses, O.*

There's nought but care on ev'ry han',
  In every hour that passes, O:
What signifies the life o' man,
  An' 'twere na for the lasses, O.

The warly race may riches chase,   worldly
  An' riches still may fly them, O;
An' tho' at last they catch them fast,
  Their hearts can ne'er enjoy them, O.

> But gie me a cannie hour at e'en,   quiet
>   My arms about my Dearie, O;
> An' warly cares, an' warly men,
>   May a' gae tapsalteerie, O!
>
> For you sae douse, ye sneer at this,   sober
>   Ye're nought but senseless asses, O:
> The wisest Man the warl' e'er saw,
>   He dearly lov'd the lasses, O.
>
> Auld Nature swears, the lovely Dears
>   Her noblest work she classes, O:
> Her prentice han' she try'd on man,
>   An' then she made the lasses, O.

ROBERT BURNS (1759–96)

Luachet is beautiful, but it wasn't her body altogether that drew me. Well, this much I can say with truth, that there is something beyond the lust of the eye and the desire of the flesh, something that is beyond the mind itself, and maybe that thing is the soul; and maybe the soul is love, and whosoever comes upon his soul is at once robbed of all thought and reason, and becomes like a flower. It was like that with me when my mother told me about our Lord Jesus's appearance in Galilee, and about his suffering and his death, for you'll remember it, my Lord Abbot, that I went to yourself and told you that the love of Jesus was in my head ever since I heard the story from my mother, and that I wanted to lose myself in love of him. And last night I was carried away just as I was on that first occasion, and I somehow cannot believe it true that my love of her will rob me of my love of Jesus, nor that her love of me will rob him of her love, for in our hearts it is all one and the same thing, and aren't we more sure that God made our hearts than of anything else? It may be, Marban continued, after he had had a look round, that I did not know this always. It may be that yesterday I would have denied the truth of what I'm now saying to you all. All the same it is the truth I'm telling you, that when the door opened and Luachet came into the room, the light of the candle that was in her hand shining on the white scriptures— The scriptures tumbled out of her hand, the old Abbot interrupted. They did not, my lord. She gave them to me, and they made plain to me that she is herself a good part of me, my scripture for ever, as long as this life lasts in me, and, if I may say it without heresy, she'll be that for the life everlasting that's to come with our Lord Jesus Christ. As good doctrine as I've heard this many a day, said the Abbot, and what's true in it has been for a long time past in the mind of God, and will be for evermore.

GEORGE MOORE (1852–1933), *A Story-Teller's Holiday*

Do but look on her eyes, they do light
    All that Love's world compriseth!
Do but look on her hair, it is bright
    As Love's star when it riseth!
Do but mark her forehead's smoother
      Than words that sooth her!
And from her arched brows, such a grace
      Sheds itself through the face,
As alone there triumphs to the life
All the gain, all the good, of the elements' strife.

Have you seen but a bright lily grow,
    Before rude hands have touched it?
Ha' you marked but the fall o' the snow
    Before the soil hath smutched it?
Ha' you felt the wool o' the beaver,
      Or swansdown ever?
Or have smelt o' the bud o' the briar,
      Or the nard in the fire?
Or have tasted the bag of the bee?
O so white! O so soft! O so sweet is she!

BEN JONSON (1573–1637), from 'A Celebration of Charis'

For lunch twelve snails, black puddings, cider (which is made here, as well as wine) and a *barquette*, under the lime tree. The temperature is right, there is a little wind, the shadowed side of the tree isn't over warm. I become too sleepy to eat, see white cloud approaching over the cliff behind sprays of elm, and shall soon be fast asleep. J. remarks that this is the way babies fall asleep on breasts, warm, full of food, and content.

Hum of an insect, hum of a car, at about the same pitch. I shut my eyes, still at table, and a red colour forms and spreads: I bend my head a little and spread a hand across my forehead, thumb one side, fingers the other, and behind the eyelids or in front of the brain the red changes to a cool dark green with vague islands of darkest blue.

I hear the clack of the sifter from the Moulin Papillon – and go to sleep.

GEOFFREY GRIGSON, *Notes from an Odd Country*

Give me, O indulgent Fate!
Give me yet, before I die,
A sweet, but absolute retreat,
'Mongst paths so lost, and trees so high,
That the world may ne'er invade,
Through such windings and such shade,
My unshaken liberty.

No intruders thither come!
Who visit, but to be from home;
None who their vain moments pass
Only studious of their glass;
News, that charm to listening ears,
That false alarm to hopes and fears,
That common theme for every fop
From the statesman to the shop,
In those coverts ne'er be spread,
Of who's deceased or who's to wed;
Be no tidings thither brought,
But silent as a midnight thought
Where the world may ne'er invade,
Be those windings, and that shade.

Courteous Fate! afford me there
A table spread without my care
With what the neighbouring fields impart,
Whose cleanliness is all their art . . .

Give me there (since Heaven has shown
It was not good to be alone)
A partner suited to my mind,
Solitary, pleased and kind,
Who, partially, may something see
Preferred to all the world in me;
Slighting, by my humble side,
Fame and splendour, wealth and pride . . .

COUNTESS OF WINCHILSEA (1661–1720),
from 'The Petition for an Absolute Retreat'

DUKE: Now my co-mates and brothers in exile,
Hath not old custom made this life more sweet
Than that of painted pomp? Are not these woods
More free from peril than the envious court?
Here feel we not the penalty of Adam,
The seasons' difference, as the icy fang
And churlish chiding of the winter's wind,
Which when it bites and blows upon my body
Even till I shrink with cold, I smile, and say
'This is no flattery. These are counsellors
That feelingly persuade me what I am'.
Sweet are the uses of adversity,
Which like the toad, ugly and venomous,
Wears yet a precious jewel in his head;
And this our life, exempt from public haunt,
Finds tongues in trees, books in the running brooks,
Sermons in stones, and good in everything.

LORD: I would not change it. Happy is your Grace,
That can translate the stubbornness of fortune
Into so quiet and so sweet a style.

DUKE: Come, shall we go and kill us venison?
And yet it irks me the poor dappled fools,
Being native burghers of this desert city,
Should in their own confines with forked heads
Have their round haunches gor'd.

WILLIAM SHAKESPEARE (1564–1616), *As You Like It*

The mellow autumn came, and with it came
The promised party, to enjoy its sweets.
The corn is cut, the manor full of game;
The pointer ranges, and the sportsman beats
In russet jacket: lynx-like is his aim;
Full grows his bag, and wonder*ful* his feats.
Ah, nutbrown partridges! Ah, brilliant pheasants!
And ah, ye poachers! – 'Tis no sport for peasants.

An English autumn, though it hath no vines,
Blushing with Bacchant coronals along
The paths, o'er which the far festoon entwines
The red grape in the sunny lands of song,
Hath yet a purchased choice of choicest wines;
The claret light, and the Madeira strong.
If Britain mourn her bleakness, we can tell her,
The very best of vineyards is the cellar.

Then, if she hath not that serene decline
Which makes the southern autumn's day appear
As if 'twould to a second spring resign
The season, rather than to winter drear,
Of in-door comforts still she hath a mine –
The sea-coal fires, the 'earliest of the year';
Without doors, too, she may compete in mellow,
As what is lost in green is gained in yellow.

LORD BYRON (1788–1824), *Don Juan*

House or window flies
These little indoor dwellers, in cottages and halls, were always entertaining to me; after dancing in the window all day from sunrise to sunset they would sip of the tea, drink of the beer, and eat of the sugar, and be welcome all summer long. They look like things of mind or fairies, and seem pleased or dull as the weather permits. In many clean cottages and genteel houses, they are allowed every liberty to creep, fly, or do as they like; and seldom or ever do wrong. In fact they are the small or dwarfish portion of our own family, and so many fairy familiars that we know and treat as one of ourselves.

JOHN CLARE (1793–1864)

Today, for the first time in my life, I have had a distinct sympathy with nature. I was lying on the top of a rock to leeward; the wind was high, and everything in motion; the branches of an oak tree were waving and murmuring to the breeze; yellow clouds, deepened by grey at the base, were rapidly floating over the western hills; the whole sky was in motion; the yellow stream below was agitated by the breeze; everything was alive, and myself part of the series of visible impressions; I should have felt pain in tearing a leaf from one of the trees.

SIR HUMPHRY DAVY (1778–1829), from a notebook

We push on. The rain has stopped, the clouds have broken; the vault of blue spreads out like a fan, the blue decomposing into the ultimate violet light which makes everything Greek seem holy, natural and familiar. In Greece one has the desire to bathe in the sky. You want to rid yourself of your clothes, take a running leap and vault into the blue. You want to float in the air like an angel or lie in the grass rigid and enjoy the cataleptic trance. Stone and sky, they marry here. It is the perpetual dawn of man's awakening.

HENRY MILLER (1891–1980), *The Colossus of Maroussi*

This darksome burn, horseback brown,
His rollrock highroad roaring down,
In coop and in comb the fleece of his foam
Flutes and low to the lake falls home.

A windpuff-bonnet of fáwn-fróth
Turns and twindles over the broth
Of a pool so pitchblack, féll-f'równing,
It rounds and rounds Despair to drowning.

Degged with dew, dappled with dew
Are the groins of the braes that the brook treads through,
Wiry heathpacks, flitches of fern,
And the beadbonny ash that sits over the burn.

What would the world be, once bereft
Of wet and of wildness? Let them be left,
O let them be left, wildness and wet;
Long live the weeds and the wilderness yet.

GERARD MANLEY HOPKINS (1844–89), 'Inversnaid'

I never wholly feel that summer is high,
However green the trees, or loud the birds,
However movelessly eye-winking herds
Stand in field ponds, or under large trees lie,
Till I do climb all cultured pastures by,
That hedged by hedgerows' studiously fretted trim,
Smile like a lady's face with lace laced prim,
And on some moor or hill that seeks the sky
Lonely and nakedly – utterly lie down,
And feel the sunshine throbbing on body and limb,
My drowsy brain in pleasant drunkenness swim,
Each rising thought sink back and dreamily drown,
Smiles creep o'er my face, and smother my lips, and cloy,
Each muscle sink to itself, and separately enjoy.

EBENEZER JONES (1820–60), 'High Summer'

Ample the air above the western peaks;
Within the peaks a silence uncompelled.
It is the hour of abnegation's self,
In clear obeisance of the mountain thrones,
And cloudless self-surrender of the skies:
The very retrospect of skiey calm,
And selfless self-approval of the hills.

WILLIAM RENTON (1875–1905), 'After Nightfall'

From yon black clump of wheat that grows
    More rank and higher than the rest,
A lark – I marked her as she rose –
    At early morning left her nest.
Her eggs were four of dusky hue,
    Blotched brown as is the very ground,
With tinges of a purply hue
    The larger ends encircling round.

Behind a clod how snug the nest
    Is in a horse's footing fixed!
Of twitch and stubbles roughly dressed,
    With roots and horsehair intermixed.
The wheat surrounds it like a bower,
    And like to thatch each bowing blade
Throws off the frequent falling shower
    – And here's an egg this morning laid!

JOHN CLARE (1793–1864), 'The Lark's Nest'

Here lies, whom hound did ne'er pursue,
    Nor swifter greyhound follow,
Whose foot ne'er tainted morning dew,
    Nor ear heard huntsman's halloo;

Old Tiney, surliest of his kind,
    Who, nursed with tender care,
And to domestic bounds confined,
    Was still a wild Jack hare.

Though duly from my hand he took
　　His pittance every night,
He did it with a jealous look,
　　And, when he could, would bite.

His diet was of wheaten bread,
　　And milk, and oats, and straw;
Thistles, or lettuces instead,
　　With sand to scour his maw.

On twigs of hawthorn he regaled,
　　On pippins' russet peel,
And, when his juicy salads failed,
　　Sliced carrot pleased him well.

A Turkey carpet was his lawn,
　　Whereon he loved to bound,
To skip and gambol like a fawn,
　　And swing his rump around.

His frisking was at evening hours,
　　For then he lost his fear,
But most before approaching showers,
　　Or when a storm drew near.

Eight years and five round-rolling moons
　　He thus saw steal away,
Dozing out all his idle noons,
　　And every night at play.

I kept him for his humour's sake,
　　For he would oft beguile
My heart of thoughts that made it ache,
　　And force me to a smile.

But now beneath his walnut shade
　　He finds his long last home,
And waits, in snug concealment laid,
　　Till gentler Puss shall come.

He, still more agéd, feels the shocks
    From which no care can save,
And, partner once of Tiney's box,
    Must soon partake his grave.

                  WILLIAM COWPER (1731–1800),
                  'Epitaph on a Hare'

Shaggy and lean and shrewd, with pointed ears
And tail cropped short, half lurcher and half cur,
His dog attends him. Close behind his heel
Now creeps he slow; and now with many a frisk
Wide-scampering snatches up the drifted snow
With ivory teeth, or ploughs it with his snout;
Then shakes his powdered coat and barks for joy.

                WILLIAM COWPER, from *The Task*

His friends he loved. His direst earthly foes –
    Cats – I believe he did but feign to hate.
My hands will miss the insinuated nose,
    Mine eyes the tail that wagged contempt at Fate.

        WILLIAM WATSON (1858–1935), 'An Epitaph'

She had a name among the children;
But no one loved though someone owned
Her, locked her out of doors at bedtime
And had her kittens duly drowned.

In Spring, nevertheless, this cat
Ate blackbirds, thrushes, nightingales,
And birds of bright voice and plume and flight,
As well as scraps from neighbours' pails.

I loathed and hated her for this;
One speckle on a thrush's breast
Was worth a million such; and yet
She lived long, till God gave her rest.

        EDWARD THOMAS (1878–1917), 'A Cat'

I searched for a woodcock I'd heard
twittering in the bluegrey caverns
of evening – a sardonic bird
with the long droll proboscis
of the born belittler – in his case
so long it belittles himself.
About starling size
he is – with like wedge-shaped wings
and tail, so that he too flutters
a faint four-pointed star
overhead where he hovers and sings
down to his maybe-more-amused-
than-moved beloved in the grass.
Anyway, at concert's end
he descends in a teetering spiral
like a drunk coming down from a box
at the opera – and after a brief silence
utters a loud piercing razzberry,
five or six times.

But, passion or parody,
his twitter among the ragged last
white clouds blown eastward
and nightward is like an English lark's,
and you'd look up too, hearing it,
to try to make him out . . . I did,
and picked up a small star all right –
so – for that demi-flash before
it registered as Vega early alight –
saw clearly a golden woodcock.
And then the very illusion's fading
made Vega seem to recede
singing into infinity. Oh,
he took me in, that parodist,
and lost me where no berries grow.

PETER KANE DUFAULT (*b*.1924),
'Notes on a Woodcock'

What things I have missed today, I know very well,
But the seeing of them each new time is miracle.
Nothing between Bredon and Dursley has
Any day yesterday's precise unpraised grace.
The changed light, or curve changed mistily,
Coppice, now bold cut, yesterday's mystery.
A sense of mornings, once seen, for ever gone,
Its own for ever: alive, dead, and my possession.

IVOR GURNEY (1890–1937), 'Yesterday Lost'

The great beauty of Poetry is, that it makes every thing, every place interesting – The palatine Venice and the abbotine Winchester are equally interesting.

JOHN KEATS (1795–1821), from a letter

I have lived in important places, times
When great events were decided, who owned
That half a rood of rock, a no-man's land
Surrounded by our pitchfork-armed claims.
I heard the Duffys shouting 'Damn your soul'
And old McCabe stripped to the waist, seen
Step the plot defying blue cast-steel –
'Here is the march along these iron stones'
That was the year of the Munich bother. Which
Was more important? I inclined
To lose my faith in Ballyrush and Gortin
Till Homer's ghost came whispering to my mind
He said: I made the Iliad from such
A local row. Gods make their own importance.

PATRICK KAVANAGH (1905–67), 'Epic'

For he defines, explains, and exalts every sweet incident of human nature; and makes dear to daily life every mystic imagination of natures greater than our own. He reconciles, while he intensifies, every virtue of domestic and monastic thought. He makes the simplest household duties sacred; and the highest religious passions, serviceable and just.

JOHN RUSKIN (1819–1900), on Giotto

Works of genius have this intrinsic property, that even when they give a perfect likeness of the nullity of things, even when they clearly demonstrate and make us feel the inevitable unhappiness of life, even when they express the most terrible despair, nevertheless to a great soul, that may even find itself in a state of utter prostration, disillusionment, futility, boredom and discouragement with life, or in the harshest and most death-dealing adversities (whether these appertain to the strong and lofty emotions, or to any other thing); they always serve as a consolation, rekindling enthusiasm, and though speaking of and portraying nothing but death, restore to it, at least for a while, the life that it had lost.

GIACOMO LEOPARDI (1798–1837), *Zibaldone*

They have charged me to be careful. I don't know to what lengths I must carry it. The fact that I have a heart inside of me makes itself felt constantly and in various ways, none of which causes me discomfort except for the anxiety of not knowing whether the signals are dangerous or not.

This mode of existence in enforced inactivity (they say I will have to consider myself ill for six months to a year) is similar to my former inactivity caused by an overabundance of strength and health; it was that stretch which prepared the way for this one.

During the early moments of danger in the hospital I accepted the thought of death with calmness and a feeling almost of bliss. I was conscious that I would not be leaving the family without funds to tide them over the initial period, and I knew they had good friends. I looked back on my life and found

nothing accidental in it – rather, a sequential logic operating
from within, which promised to perpetuate itself.

The force of this logic told even in my moods at those
moments. I rejoiced that on being brought to the hospital at
night I was put to bed in a corridor overcrowded with a
miscellany of mortals at death's door, and I thanked almighty
God for having created me an artist, capable of being moved to
tears of triumph and ecstasy by the contemplation of form in all
its manifestations – the city rising outside the windows, the
juxtaposition of light and shadow, of life and death.

BORIS PASTERNAK (1890–1960), from a letter

At certain moments, always unforeseen, I become happy, most
commonly when at hazard I have opened some book of verse.
Sometimes it is my own verse when, instead of discovering new
technical flaws, I read with all the excitement of the first
writing. Perhaps I am sitting in some crowded restaurant, the
open book beside me, or closed, my excitement having over-
brimmed the page. I look at the strangers near as if I had known
them all my life, and it seems strange that I cannot speak to
them: everything fills me with affection, I have no longer any
fears or any needs; I do not even remember that this happy
mood must come to an end. It seems as if the vehicle had
suddenly grown pure and far extended and so luminous that
the images from *Anima Mundi*, embodied there and drunk with
that sweetness, would, like a country drunkard who has thrown
a wisp into his own thatch, burn up time.

It may be an hour before the mood passes, but latterly I seem
to understand that I enter upon it the moment I cease to hate. I
think the common condition of our life is hatred – I know that
this is so with me – irritation with public or private events or
persons. There is no great matter in forgetfulness of servants, or
the delays of tradesmen, but how forgive the ill-breeding of
Carlyle, or the rhetoric of Swinburne, or that woman who
murmurs over the dinner-table the opinion of her daily paper?
And only a week ago last Sunday, I hated the spaniel who
disturbed a partridge on her nest, a trout who took my bait and
yet broke away unhooked. The books say that our happiness

comes from the opposite of hate, but I am not certain, for we may love unhappily. And plainly, when I have closed a book too stirred to go on reading, and in those brief intense visions of sleep, I have something about me that, though it makes me love, is more like innocence.

W. B. YEATS (1865–1939), *Mythologies*

My fiftieth year had come and gone,
I sat, a solitary man,
In a crowded London shop,
An open book and empty cup
On the marble table-top.

While on the shop and street I gazed
My body of a sudden blazed;
And twenty minutes more or less
It seemed, so great my happiness,
That I was blesséd and could bless.

W. B. YEATS, from 'Vacillation'

AUGUST, 1888

This restaurant where I am is very queer; it is completely grey; the floor is of grey bitumen like a street pavement, grey paper on the walls, green blinds always drawn, a big green curtain in front of the door which is always open, to stop the dust coming in. Just as it is it is a Velasquez grey – like in the *Spinning Women* – and the very narrow, very fierce ray of sunlight through a blind, like the one that crosses Velasquez's picture, even that is not wanting. Little tables, of course, with white cloths. And behind this room in Velasquez grey you see the old kitchen, as clean as a Dutch kitchen, with floor of bright red bricks, green vegetables, oak chest, the kitchen range with shining brass things and blue and white tiles, and the big fire a clear orange. And then there are two women who wait, both in grey, a little like that picture of Prévost's you have in your place – you could compare it point for point.

In the kitchen, an old woman and a short, fat servant also in grey, black, white. I don't know if I describe it clearly enough to you, but it's here, and it's pure Velasquez.

In front of the restaurant there is a covered court, paved with red brick, and on the walls wild vine, convolvulus and creepers.

It is the real old Provençal still, while the other restaurants are so much modelled on Paris that *even when they have no kind of concierge whatever*, there's his booth just the same and the notice 'Apply to the Concierge!'

It isn't always all vibrant here. Thus I saw a stable with four coffee-coloured cows, and a calf of the same colour. The stable bluish white hung with spiders' webs, the cows very clean and very beautiful, and a great green curtain in the doorway to keep out flies and dust.

Grey again – Velasquez's grey.

There was such quiet in it – the café au lait and tobacco colour of the cows' hides, with the soft bluish grey white of the walls, the green hanging and the sparkling sunny golden-green outside to make a startling contrast. So you see there's something still to be done, quite different from anything I have done up to now.

I must go and work. I saw another very quiet and lovely thing the other day, a girl with a coffee-tinted skin if I remember rightly, ash blond hair, grey eyes, a print bodice of pale rose under which you could see the breasts, shapely, firm and small. This against the emerald leaves of some fig trees. A woman of the real country sort, every line of her virgin.

It isn't altogether impossible that I shall get her to pose in the open air, and her mother too – a gardener's wife – earth coloured, dressed just then in soiled yellow and faded blue.

The girl's coffee-tinted complexion was darker than the rose of her bodice.

The mother was stunning, the figure in dirty yellow and faded blue thrown up in strong sunlight against a square of brilliant flowers, snow white and lemon-yellow. A perfect Van der Meer of Delft, you see.

It's not a bad place, the south. A handshake.

Yours,
Vincent

SEPTEMBER, 1888

I do strongly ask you to keep my studies of this place as open to the air as possible, because they are not yet thoroughly dry. If they remain shut up or in the dark the colours will get devalued. So the portrait of 'The Young Girl', 'The Harvest' (a wide landscape with the ruin in the background and the line of the Alpilles), the little 'Seascape', the 'Garden' with the weeping tree and clumps of conifers, if you could put these on stretchers it would be well. I am rather keen on those. You will easily see by the *drawing* of the little seascape that it is the most thought out.

I am having two oak frames made for my new peasant's head and for my Poet study. Oh, my dear boy, sometimes I know so well what I want. I can very well do without God both in my life and in my painting, but I cannot, ill as I am, do without something which is greater than I, which is my life – the power to create.

And if, defrauded of the power to create physically, a man tries to create thoughts in place of children, he is still very much part of humanity.

And in a picture I want to say something comforting as music is comforting. I want to paint men and women with that something of the eternal which the halo used to symbolize, and which we seek to confer by the actual radiance and vibration of our colourings.

VINCENT VAN GOGH, from letters to his brother

The future of poetry is immense, because in poetry, where it is worthy of its high destinies, our race, as time goes on, will find an ever surer and surer stay. There is not a creed which is not shaken, not an accredited dogma which is not shown to be questionable, not a received tradition which does not threaten to dissolve. Our religion has materialised itself in the fact, in the supposed fact; it has attached its emotion to the fact, and now the fact is failing it. But for poetry the idea is everything; the rest is a world of illusion, of divine illusion. Poetry attaches its emotion to the idea; the idea *is* the fact. The strongest part of our religion to-day is its unconscious poetry.

MATTHEW ARNOLD (1822–88), 'The Study of Poetry'

I was unlike others of my generation in one thing only. I am very religious, and deprived by Huxley and Tyndall, whom I detested, of the simple-minded religion of my childhood, I had made a new religion, almost an infallible Church of poetic tradition, of a fardel of stories, and of personages, and of emotions, inseparable from their first expression, passed on from generation to generation by poets and painters with some help from philosophers and theologians. I wished for a world where I could discover this tradition perpetually, and not in pictures and in poems only, but in tiles round the chimney-piece and in the hangings that kept out the draught. I had even created a dogma: 'Because those imaginary people are created out of the deepest instinct of man, to be his measure and his norm, whatever I can imagine those mouths speaking may be the nearest I can go to truth'. When I listened they seemed always to speak of one thing only: they, their loves, every incident of their lives, were steeped in the supernatural. Could even Titian's *Ariosto* that I loved beyond other portraits have its grave look, as if waiting for some perfect final event, if the painters before Titian had not learned portraiture while paint-ing into the corner of compositions full of saints and Madonnas their kneeling patrons? At seventeen years old I was already an old-fashioned brass cannon full of shot, and nothing had kept me from going off but a doubt as to my capacity to shoot straight.

W. B. YEATS, Autobiographies

. . .   And now in age I bud again,
After so many deaths I live and write;
    I once more smell the dew and rain,
And relish versing: O my only light,
         It cannot be
         That I am he
On whom thy tempests fell last night. . .

GEORGE HERBERT (1593–1633),
from 'The Flower'

A thousand things make one compose or not compose: composition seems to keep alive in me a *cheerfulness* – a sort of Tuchtigkeit, or natural soundness and valiancy, which I think the present age is fast losing – this is why I like it.

I am glad you like the Gipsy Scholar – but what does it *do* for you? Homer *animates* – Shakespeare *animates* – in its poor way I think 'Sohrab and Rustum' *animates* – the Gipsy Scholar at best awakens a pleasing melancholy. But this is not what we want.

> The complaining millions of men
> Darken in labour and pain –

what they want is something to *animate* and *ennoble* them – not merely to add zest to their melancholy or grace to their dreams. – I believe a feeling of this kind is the basis of my nature – and of my poetics.

MATTHEW ARNOLD, from a letter

MIDNIGHT, 5-9-36
Machiavelli, in a passage which I cannot find, and the Chinese sages agree that certain formalities are necessary before reading or writing can be properly pursued. M. dressed himself after his work in the country, and lit wax candles. The Chinese 'sit down before a bright window, at a clean table, burning a stick of incense to dispel anxiety, in order that the fine verses and excellent concepts should take shape'. How amused and contemptuous I should once have been of this! I thought I could read or write properly anywhere; yet 'if one does not act in this way inspiration will soon be restrained, distracted, dulled or hindered; and how would one then represent the appearances of things and emotions?' Lust, fun, kindness, and fear are my own restraints and distractions: fear the strongest of the four, for the collapse of civilisation seems to eat up from below into anything I do. A clean table and proper lighting makes me solider, I find. Tonight I have swept all the rubbish off my board and read some of Oedipus Tyrannus with only the lamp and two vases in sight. One vase has four roses, the other a spray of oak leaves: the acorns when the sun falls on them, have a blue bloom.

E. M. FORSTER (1879–1970), *Commonplace Book*

Whenever I find myself growing vapourish, I rouse myself, wash and put on a clean shirt brush my hair and clothes, tie my shoestrings neatly and in fact adonize as I were going out – then all clean and comfortable I sit down to write. This I find the greatest relief.

JOHN KEATS, from a letter

Reasons briefly set down by the author to persuade everyone to learn to sing:

First, it is a knowledge easily taught, and quickly learned, where there is a good master and an apt scholar.

2. The exercise of singing is delightful to Nature, and good to preserve the health of man.

3. It doth strengthen all parts of the breast, and open the pipes.

4. It is a singular good remedy for a stutting and stammering in the speech.

5. It is the best means to procure a perfect pronunciation, and to make a good orator.

6. It is the only way to know where Nature hath bestowed the benefit of a good voice; which gift is so rare, as there is not one among a thousand that hath it; and in many, that excellent gift is lost, because they want Art to express Nature.

7. There is not any music of instruments whatsoever, comparable to that which is made of the voices of men, where the voices are good, and the same well sorted and ordered.

8. The better the voice is, the meeter it is to honour and serve God therewith; and the voice of man is chiefly to be employed to that end.

Since singing is so good a thing
I wish all men would learn to sing.

*Omnis spiritus laudet Dominum**

WILLIAM BYRD (1543–1623)

* *Let everything that hath breath praise the Lord*

All we have willed or hoped or dreamed of good, shall exist;
  Not its semblance, but itself; no beauty, nor good, nor
      power
Whose voice has gone forth, but each survives for the
        melodist
  When eternity affirms the conception of an hour.
The high that proved too high, the heroic for earth too hard,
  The passion that left the ground to lose itself in the sky,
Are music sent up to God by the lover and the bard;
  Enough that He heard it once: we shall hear it by-and-by.

And what is our failure here but a triumph's evidence
  For the fulness of the days? Have we withered or agonized?
Why else was the pause prolonged but that singing might
      issue thence?
  Why rushed the discords in, but that harmony should be
      prized?
Sorrow is hard to bear, and doubt is slow to clear,
  Each sufferer says his say, his scheme of the weal and woe:
But God has a few of us whom He whispers in the ear;
  The rest may reason and welcome: 'tis we musicians know.

Well, it is earth with me; silence resumes her reign:
  I will be patient and proud, and soberly acquiesce.
Give me the keys. I feel for the common chord again,
  Sliding by semitones, till I sink to the minor – yes,
And I blunt it into a ninth, and I stand on alien ground,
  Surveying a while the heights I rolled from into the deep;
Which, hark, I have dared and done, for my resting-place is
      found,
  The C Major of this life: so, now I will try to sleep.

ROBERT BROWNING (1812–89), from 'Abt Vogler'

AGE

Age: the elderly can sometimes look on the present with a jaundiced eye. Therefore Castiglione's logic, that if all fathers were better than their sons in every generation, no further deterioration would be possible, ought to be consoling – if the fathers can believe it.

The American poet John Berryman said he'd scoured the wise books of the world and found no more useful remark than Maurice Chevalier's when he was asked how he felt about growing old, 'It's not so bad if you consider the alternative.' Perhaps Berryman had not come across Cicero's cheerful defence of any old person, 'he is better off than his juniors; since what they are hoping for he has actually achieved: they want long lives, and he has had one'.

E. M. Forster describes his unfrightening experience of nearly dying. There follows a little group of love in age, and George Herbert brings in the idea that age means rest, and rest is good. A few more celebrations of rest are concluded by Dr Johnson's resistance to any such notion.

I have many times asked myself, not without wonder, the source of a certain error which, since it is committed by all the old without exception, can be believed to be proper and natural to man: namely, that they nearly all praise the past and blame the present, revile our actions and behaviour and everything which they themselves did not do when they were young, and affirm, too, that every good custom and way of life, every virtue and, in short, all things imaginable are always going from bad to worse. And truly it seems against all reason and a cause for astonishment that maturity of age, which, with its long experience, in all other respects usually perfects a man's judgement, in this matter corrupts it so much that he does not realize that, if the world were always growing worse and if fathers were generally better than their sons, we would long since have become so rotten that no further deterioration would be possible.

CASTIGLIONE (1478–1529), *The Book of the Courtier*

"'Twas not so in *my* time,' surly Grumio exclaims,
When our fancies, and fashions, and follies he blames:
But your times, and our times, and all times, old Bluff!
Can show fancies, and fashions, and follies enough!
Your taste was the formal, as ours is the flimsy:
You made wisdom grimace; we make elegance whimsy.
'Tis all the same foppery, dressed different ways!
Yours was yesterday's nonsense; and ours is today's!

SAMUEL BISHOP (1731–95), 'Epigram'

Between thirty and forty, one is distracted by the Five Lusts;
Between seventy and eighty, one is a prey to a hundred
   diseases.
But from fifty to sixty one is free from all ills;
Calm and still – the heart enjoys rest.
I have put behind me Love and Greed; I have done with
   Profit and Fame;
I am still short of illness and decay and far from decrepit age.
Strength of limb I still possess to seek the rivers and hills;
Still my heart has spirit enough to listen to flutes and strings.
At leisure I open new wine and taste several cups;
Drunken I recall old poems and sing a whole volume.
Mēng-tē has asked for a poem and herewith I exhort him
Not to complain of three-score, 'the time of obedient ears'.*

PO CHÜ-I (773–846), 'On being Sixty' tr. Arthur Waley

* Confucius said that it was not till sixty that his ears obeyed him. This age was called
therefore 'the time of obedient ears'.

Stella's Birthday, 1727

> This day, whate'er the Fates decree,
> Shall still be kept with joy by me;
> This day then, let us not be told
> That you are sick, and I grown old,
> Nor think on our approaching ills,
> And talk of spectacles and pills;
> Tomorrow will be time enough
> To hear such mortifying stuff.
> Yet since from reason may be brought
> A better and more pleasing thought,
> Which can in spite of all decays
> Support a few remaining days:
> From not the gravest of Divines
> Accept for once some serious lines.
>
> Although we now can form no more
> Long schemes of life, as heretofore,
> Yet you, while Time is running fast,
> Can look with joy on what is past.

Were future happiness and pain
A mere contrivance of the brain,
As atheists argue, to entice
And fit their proselytes for vice
(The only comfort they propose,
To have companions in their woes);
Grant this the case, yet sure 'tis hard
That Virtue, styled its own reward,
And by all sages understood
To be the chief of human good,
Should acting, die, nor leave behind
Some lasting pleasure in the mind,
Which by remembrance will assuage
Grief, sickness, poverty and age;
And strongly shoot a radiant dart
To shine through life's declining part.

Say, Stella, feel you no content,
Reflecting on a life well spent?
Your skilful hand employed to save
Despairing wretches from the grave,
And then supporting from your store
Those whom you dragged from death before
(So Providence on mortals waits,
Preserving what it first creates);
Your generous boldness to defend
An innocent and absent friend;
That courage which can make you just
To Merit humbled in the dust;
The detestation you express
For Vice in all its glittering dress;
That patience under torturing pain,
Where stubborn Stoics would complain.

Must these like empty shadows pass,
Or forms reflected in a glass?
Or mere chimeras in the mind
That fly and leave no marks behind?
Does not the body thrive and grow

By food of twenty years ago?
And had it not been still supplied
It must a thousand times have died.
Then, who with reason can maintain
That no effects of food remain?
And is not virtue in mankind
The nutriment that feeds the mind?
Upheld by each good action past,
And still continued by the last;
Then, who with reason can pretend
That all effects of virtue end?

Believe me Stella, when you show
That true contempt for things below,
Nor prize your life for other ends
Than merely to oblige your friends,
Your former actions claim their part,
And join to fortify your heart.
For Virtue in her daily race,
Like Janus, bears a double face;
Looks back with joy where she has gone,
And therefore goes with courage on.
She at your sickly couch will wait,
And guide you to a better state.

O then, whatever Heaven intends,
Take pity on your pitying friends;
Nor let your ills affect your mind
To fancy they can be unkind.
Me, surely me, you ought to spare,
Who gladly would your sufferings share,
Or give my scrap of life to you
And think it far beneath your due:
You, to whose care so oft I owe
That I'm alive to tell you so.

JONATHAN SWIFT (1667–1745)

'Sir, I love the acquaintance of young people; because, in the first place, I don't like to think myself growing old. In the next place, young acquaintances must last longer, if they do last; and then, Sir, young men have more virtue than old men; they have more generous sentiments in every respect. I love the young dogs of this age, they have more wit and humour and knowledge of life than we had; but then the dogs are not so good scholars. Sir, in my early years I read very hard. It is a sad reflection, but a true one, that I knew almost as much at eighteen as I do now. My judgement, to be sure, was not so good; but, I had all the facts. I remember very well, when I was at Oxford, an old gentleman said to me, "Young man, ply your book diligently now, and acquire a stock of knowledge; for when years come upon you, you will find that poring upon books will be but an irksome task."'

SAMUEL JOHNSON (1709–84), aged 55

Resolutions When I Come to Be Old.
Not to marry a young woman.
Not to keep young company unless they really desire it.
Not to be peevish or morose, or suspicious.
Not to scorn present ways, or wits, or fashions, or men, or
    war, etc.
Not to be fond of children, or let them come near me hardly.
Not to tell the same story over and over to the same people.
Not to be covetous.
Not to neglect decency, or cleanliness, for fear of falling into
    nastiness.
Not to be over severe with young people, but give allowances
    for their youthful follies, and weaknesses.
Not to be influenced by, or give ear to knavish tattling
    servants, or others.
Not to be too free of advice, nor trouble any but those that
    desire it.
To desire some good friends to inform me which of these
    Resolutions I break, or neglect, and wherein; and reform
    accordingly.
Not to talk much, nor of myself.

Not to boast of my former beauty, or strength, or favour with
  ladies, etc.
Not to hearken to flatteries, nor conceive I can be beloved by
  a young woman.
Not to be positive or opiniative.
Not to set up for observing all these Rules, for fear I should
  observe none.

JONATHAN SWIFT (1667–1745), aged 32

Thoughts on Various Subjects, No. 24
  No wise man ever wished to be younger.

JONATHAN SWIFT

'Another sandwich!' said the King.
'There's nothing but hay left now,' the Messenger said,
peeping into the bag.
'Hay, then,' the King murmured in a faint whisper.
Alice was glad to see that it revived him a good deal. 'There's
nothing like eating hay when you're faint,' he remarked to her,
as he munched away.
'I should think throwing cold water over you would be
better,' Alice suggested: '– or some sal-volatile.'
'I didn't say there was nothing *better*,' the King replied. 'I
said there was nothing *like* it.' Which Alice did not venture to
deny.

LEWIS CARROLL (1832–98), *Through the Looking-Glass*

In fact, here I am these current years 1890 and 1891, (each
successive fortnight getting stiffer and stuck deeper) much like
some hard-cased dilapidated grim ancient shell-fish or time-
banged conch (no legs, utterly non-locomotive) cast up high
and dry on the shore-sands, helpless to move anywhere –
nothing left but behave myself quiet, and while away the days
yet assigned, and discover if there is anything for the said grim
and time-banged conch to be got at last out of inherited good
spirits and primal buoyant centre-pulses down there deep

somewhere within his gray-blurred old shell. . . . (Reader, you must allow a little fun here – for one reason there are too many of the following poemets about death, etc., and for another the passing hours (July 5, 1890) are so sunny-fine. And old as I am I feel today almost a part of some frolicsome wave, or for sporting yet like a kid or kitten – probably a streak of physical adjustment and perfection here and now. I believe I have it in me perennially anyhow.)

WALT WHITMAN (1819–92),
Preface to the last edition of *Leaves of Grass*, 1891

It is time to be old,
To take in sail:
The god of bounds,
Who sets to seas a shore,
Came to me in his fatal rounds,
And said, 'No more!
No farther shoot
Thy broad ambitious branches, and thy root.
Fancy departs: no more invent;
Contract thy firmament
To compass of a tent.
There's not enough for this and that,
Make thy option which of two;
Economize the failing river,
Not the less revere the Giver,
Leave the many and hold the few.
Timely wise accept the terms,
Soften the fall with wary foot;
A little while
Still plan and smile,
And – fault of novel germs –
Mature the unfallen fruit.
Curse, if thou wilt, thy sires,
Bad husbands of their fires,
Who, when they gave thee breath,
Failed to bequeath
The needful sinew stark as once,

The Baresark marrow to thy bones,
But left a legacy of ebbing veins,
Inconstant heat and nerveless reins –
Amid the Muses, left thee deaf and dumb,
Amid the gladiators, halt and numb.'

As the bird trims her to the gale,
I trim myself to the storm of time,
I man the rudder, reef the sail,
Obey the voice at eve obeyed at prime:
'Lowly faithful, banish fear,
Right onward drive unharmed;
The port, well worth the cruise, is near,
And every wave is charmed.'

RALPH WALDO EMERSON (1803–92), 'Terminus'

Without stirring abroad
One can know the whole world;
Without looking out of the window
One can see the way of heaven.
The further one goes
The less one knows.
Therefore the sage knows without having to stir,
Identifies without having to see,
Accomplishes without having to act.

LAO–TSE, *Tao Te Ching*, c.400 BC

Ackerley, Joe, sentence in letter from:

The days potter by here much the same; sometimes the sad
sound of their ticking feet gets into my ears as they disappear
into history, carrying nothing in their delicate hands but a
yawn.

Can the day that produced such a sentence be lost?

E. M. FORSTER (1879–1970), *Commonplace Book*

Entering today my eightieth year, after a late breakfast
I settle to presents, and now to writing a poem. It is a day
Recapitulating my years. So far we have had sleet, snow,
Coldest wind from far north, draughts sneaking
Through cracks and positively shaking cut flowers
In their vases, and sunshine, and glittering leaves.
   I have in the past seen flesh which was pink and warm
Turn green and cold, and this morning tears have rolled
    from me
So that I could not see. To-day the colour I think of is blue.
Not only because blue bays of sky are occurring
Between black shores of cloud. Various things come
Into thought, and these include blue doves
Of columbine hanging in damp grass, and scent
Of primroses and pale yolk and fluff of scented mimosa
    around and above
Fallen columns, and Thomas Nashe, son of a neighbouring
    parson
Whom my ancestors undoubtedly knew, settling in his day
To writing – how, when and where, and why
In particular, that dust has closed Helen's eye
And Queens have died young and fair. Oddly
In London's *Evening Standard* yesterday a barbarous female
Wrote about Thomas Nashe (friend of Shakespeare)
And she talked only of violence and brothels and forgot
To mention that poem.
   May be what I am thinking of to-day
Strictly is selfish: but on a birthday I am entitled
To think of myself and be thankful; and await a call from
My daughter. After all how could I help being born, and
    having
Been born, should I not think the best of life so conferred,
In recollection? Even for others.
   There are stuffy short poets whose pretentious
Writings in the human cause fill me with dismay.
To-day let me forget them, and exclude them. Moments ago
Life seemed a driving hell of small flakes of pitiless
Snow. Each car that passes is white-roofed, now changes
Are so sudden, under a cold Pacific; and so far, so far

I have survived; and though I may not see them again,
It won't be long now before primrose-scents of mimosa
At Salamis and curdled primroses along hedges
Of Cornwall recur, and bells peal at Easter for
Marriages, though muffled they peal also for dying,
And, for Time, the Maxingona booms over Venice.
O benedicite, omnia opera. O blue doves
Sipping in that wet bowl of grasses in the sudden
Glittering corner. O if for a life, if for a moment, still
Benedicite, omnia opera.

GEOFFREY GRIGSON (1905–85), 'Entering My Eightieth Year'

My whole life can be divided in two halves; the first up to the
time I was forty; and the second *after* the time I was forty.
During the first half I struggled desperately to evoke and to
arrange my feelings according to what I admired in my favourite books; but during the second half I struggled to find out
what my real feelings were and to refine upon them and to
balance them and to harmonize them, according to no one's
method but my own.

JOHN COWPER POWYS (1872–1963), *Autobiography*

At times I question myself as to whether I have become a better
person than I was as a young man, but the right answer always
eludes me. At any rate, the question is rather pointless. We are
what we are, and if we are not then the best thing we can hope
for is to become, or rather rebecome, what we are, which
excludes the unnecessary quest for improvement. I don't think
I have improved myself to any measurable extent, but I have
become a little more myself than I was.

ALFRED PERLÈS (1897–1990), *A Snail's Pace Suits Me Fine*

I turn away and shut the door, and on the stair
Wonder how many times I could have proved my worth
In something that all others understand or share;
But O! ambitious heart, had such a proof drawn forth
A company of friends, a conscience set at ease,
It had but made us pine the more. The abstract joy,
The half-read wisdom of daemonic images,
Suffice the ageing man as once the growing boy.

W. B. YEATS (1865–1939), from 'Meditations in Time of Civil War'

But to return to the imminence of death. This is not a fault to blame on age, since you can see that youth may suffer from the same disability. The loss of my dear son, and of your two brothers, Scipio – both destined for brilliant careers – has underlined for both of us that death comes to all ages alike. Certainly you can argue that young men are entitled to hope for long lives, whereas old men are not. But such hopes are misguided, since it is unintelligent to mistake certainty for uncertainty, and untruth for truth.

The objector may go on to say that an old man has nothing even to hope for. Still, he is better off than his juniors, since what they are hoping for he has actually achieved: they want long lives, and he has had one.

CICERO (106–43 BC), *On Old Age*

Nearly Dying: meant to record this sooner. No pain, no fear, no thoughts of eternity, infinity, fate, love, sin, humanity, or any of the usuals. Only weakness, and too weak to be aware of anything but weakness. 'I shan't be here if I get weaker than this' was the nearest approach to a thought. I know that Bob and May were to my right and left – they had been summoned by the police and arrived about 4 – and was not surprised and liked touching them: Bob's little finger pressed mine and pursued it when it shifted. This I shall never forget. Blood – 3 pts? of it – dripped from a high-suspended ampoule into the back of my right hand. I liked watching this later, or the white saline that sometimes took its place – bubbles ascended

through this later and demonstrated that it was descending. –
But this diverts me from the 'nearly-dying' moment that I am
trying to recapture; for then I had no awareness of anything
except weakness. I may not have watched the ampoule until the
next day. It was certainly then that I made Bob and May laugh
by telling them an anecdote about Ben which I knew would
amuse them. The Sister pounced outraged. 'I must have my
little joke' I said, conciliatory.

The experience has convinced me that death is nothing if one
can approach it as such. I was just a tiny night-light, suffocated
in its own wax, and on the point of expiring. I may feel differently when my death really succeeds, and others may feel
different. I didn't find my mother different – she just stopped
eating some nice stew which Agnes had made her and with
which I was feeding her, and showed no perturbation although
she had told me half an hour before that I should not have her
long.

E. M. FORSTER (1879–1970), *Commonplace Book*

Believe me, if all those endearing young charms,
    Which I gaze on so fondly to-day,
Were to change by to-morrow, and fleet in my arms,
    Like fairy-gifts fading away,
Thou wouldst still be adored, as this moment thou art
    Let thy loveliness fade as it will,
And around the dear ruin each wish of my heart
    Would entwine itself verdantly still.

It is not while beauty and youth are thine own,
    And thy cheeks unprofaned by a tear,
That the fervor and faith of a soul can be known,
    To which time will but make thee more dear;
No, the heart that has truly loved never forgets,
    But as truly loves on to the close,
As the sun-flower turns on her god, when he sets,
    The same look which she turned when he rose.

THOMAS MOORE (1779–1852)

Ancient Person, for whom I
All the flattering youth defy,
Long be it ere thou grow old,
Aching, shaking, crazy, cold,
But still continue as thou art,
Ancient Person of my Heart.

On thy withered lips and dry
Which like barren furrows lie
Brooding kisses I will pour,
Shall thy youthful heart restore.
Such kind showers in autumn fall,
And a second spring recall,
Nor from thee will ever part,
Ancient Person of my Heart.

Thy nobler part, which but to name
In our sex would be counted shame,
By ages' frozen grasp possessed
From their ice shall be released;
And soothed by my reviving hand,
In former warmth and vigour stand.
All a lover's wish can reach
For thy joy my love shall teach;
And for thy pleasure shall improve
All that art can add to love.
Yet still I love thee without art,
Ancient Person of my Heart.

EARL OF ROCHESTER (1647–80), 'A Song of
a Young Lady to her Ancient Lover'

His golden locks time hath to silver turned.
    Oh, time too swift! Oh, swiftness never ceasing!
His youth 'gainst time and age hath ever spurned,
    But spurned in vain; youth waneth by increasing:
Beauty, strength, youth, are flowers but fading seen;
Duty, faith, love, are roots, and ever green.

His helmet now shall make a hive for bees;
  And, lovers' sonnets turned to holy psalms,
A man-at-arms must now serve on his knees,
  And feed on prayers, which are age's alms:
But though from court to cottage he depart,
His saint is sure of his unspotted heart.

And when he saddest sits in homely cell,
  He'll teach his swains this carol for a song:
'Blest be the hearts that wish my sovereign well,
  Curst be the souls that think her any wrong.'
Goddess, allow this agéd man his right,
To be your beadsman now, that was your knight.

GEORGE PEELE (1556–96)

That time of year thou mayst in me behold
When yellow leaves, or none, or few, do hang
Upon those boughs which shake against the cold;
Bare ruined choirs, where late the sweet birds sang.
In me thou seest the twilight of such day
As after sunset fadeth in the west,
Which by and by black night doth take away:
Death's second self that seals up all in rest.
In me thou seest the glowing of such fire
That on the ashes of his youth doth lie,
As the death-bed whereon it must expire,
Consumed with that which it was nourished by.
This thou perceiv'st, which makes thy love more strong,
To love that well, which thou must leave ere long.

WILLIAM SHAKESPEARE (1564–1616)

  When God at first made man,
  Having a glass of blessings standing by,
  Let us (said he) pour on him all we can;
  Let the world's riches, which disperséd lie,
    Contract into a span.

So strength first made a way;
Then beauty flowed, then wisdom, honour, pleasure;
When almost all was out, God made a stay,
Perceiving that alone of all his treasure
    Rest in the bottom lay.

For if I should (said he)
Bestow this jewel also on my creature,
He would adore my gifts instead of me,
And rest in Nature, not the God of Nature:
    So both should losers be.

Yet let him keep the rest,
But keep them with repining restlessness;
Let him be rich and weary, that at least,
If goodness lead him not, yet weariness
    May toss him to my breast.

        GEORGE HERBERT (1593–1633), 'The Pulley'

Under the wide and starry sky,
Dig the grave and let me lie.
Glad did I live and gladly die,
    And I laid me down with a will.

This be the verse you grave for me:
Here he lies where he longed to be;
Home is the sailor, home from sea,
    And the hunter home from the hill.

      ROBERT LOUIS STEVENSON (1850–94), 'Requiem'

Never weather-beaten sail more willing bent to shore,
Never tired pilgrim's limbs affected slumber more,
Than my wearied spright now longs to fly, out of my
  troubled breast:
O come quickly, sweetest Lord, and take my soul to rest.

Ever-blooming are the joys of heaven's high paradise,
Cold age deafs not there our ears, nor vapour dims our eyes;
Glory there the sun outshines, whose beams the blessèd only see
O come quickly, glorious Lord, and raise my spright to thee.

EDMUND CAMPION (1567–1620)

For the Bed at Kelmscott
The wind's on the wold
And the night is a-cold,
And Thames runs chill
Twixt mead and hill,
But kind and dear
Is the old house here,
And my heart is warm
Midst winter's harm.
Rest, then and rest,
And think of the best
Twixt summer and spring
When all birds sing
In the town of the tree,
And ye lie in me
And scarce dare move
Lest earth and its love
Should fade away
Ere the full of the day.
I am old and have seen
Many things that have been,
Both grief and peace,
And wane and increase.
No tale I tell
Of ill or well,
But this I say,
Night treadeth on day,
And for worst and best
Right good is rest.

WILLIAM MORRIS (1834–96)

Ill health – which had granted me quite a long spell of leave – has attacked me without warning again. 'What kind of ill health?' you'll be asking. And well you may, for there isn't a single kind I haven't experienced. There's one particular ailment, though, for which I've always been singled out, so to speak. I see no reason why I should call it by its Greek name,* difficulty in breathing being a perfectly good way of describing it. Its onslaught is of very brief duration – like a squall, it is generally over within the hour. One could hardly, after all, expect anyone to keep on drawing his last breath for long, could one? I've been visited by all the troublesome or dangerous complaints there are, and none of them, in my opinion, is more unpleasant than this one – which is hardly surprising, is it, when you consider that with anything else you're merely ill, while with this you're constantly at your last gasp? This is why doctors have nicknamed it 'rehearsing death', since sooner or later the breath does just what it has been trying to do all those times. Do you imagine that as I write this I must be feeling in high spirits at having escaped this time? No, it would be just as absurd for me to feel overjoyed at its being over – as if this meant I was a healthy man again – as it would be for a person to think he has won his case on obtaining an extension of time before trial.

Even as I fought for breath, though, I never ceased to find comfort in cheerful and courageous reflections. 'What's this?' I said. 'So death is having all these tries at me, is he? Let him, then! I had a try at him a long while ago myself.' 'When was this?' you'll say. Before I was born. Death is just not being. What that is like I know already. It will be the same after me as it was before me. If there is any torment in the later state, there must also have been torment in the period before we saw the light of day; yet we never felt conscious of any distress then. I ask you, wouldn't you say that anyone who took the view that a lamp was worse off when it was put out than it was before it was lit was an utter idiot? We, too, are lit and put out. We suffer somewhat in the intervening period, but at either end of it there is a deep tranquillity. For, unless I'm mistaken, we are wrong,

* i.e. its medical name, *asthma*

my dear Lucilius, in holding that death follows after, when in fact it precedes as well as succeeds. Death is all that was before us. What does it matter, after all, whether you cease to be or never begin, when the result of either is that you do not exist?

I kept on talking to myself in these and similar terms – silently, needless to say, words being out of the question. Then little by little the affliction in my breathing, which was coming to be little more than a panting now, came on at longer intervals and slackened away. It has lasted on, all the same, and in spite of the passing of this attack, my breathing is not yet coming naturally. I feel a sort of catch and hesitation in it. Let it do as it pleases, though, so long as the sighs aren't heartfelt. You can feel assured on my score of this: I shall not be afraid when the last hour comes – I'm already prepared, not planning as much as a day ahead. The man, though, whom you should admire and imitate is the one who finds it a joy to live and in spite of that is not reluctant to die. For where's the virtue in going out when you're really being thrown out? And yet there is this virtue about my case: I'm in the process of being thrown out, certainly, but the manner of it is as if I were going out. And the reason why it never happens to a wise man is that being thrown out signifies expulsion from a place one is reluctant to depart from, and there is nothing the wise man does reluctantly. He escapes necessity because he wills what necessity is going to force on him.

SENECA (*c*.4 BC–AD 65)

As Johnson had now very faint hopes of recovery, and as Mrs. Thrale was no longer devoted to him, it might have been supposed that he would naturally have chosen to remain in the comfortable house of his beloved wife's daughter, and end his life where he began it. But there was in him an animated and lofty spirit, and however complicated diseases might depress ordinary mortals, all who saw him beheld and acknowledged the *invictum animum Catonis*.* Such was his intellectual ardour

* the stubborn spirit of Cato.

even at this time, that he said to one friend, 'Sir, I look upon every day to be lost, in which I do not make a new acquaintance'; and to another, when talking of his illness, 'I will be conquered; I will not capitulate.'

JAMES BOSWELL, *Life of Samuel Johnson*, year 1784

LAMENT

If Dr Johnson is right, and 'sorrow is remedied by exercise and motion', then the exercise of putting sorrow into words is a form of remedy.

Nashe laments for all the conditions of life. Byron's poem is one of regret, rather than lament, but is an elegant acknowledgement of the erosions of time, and elegance is a form of defiance.

Melville expresses remorse for what no longer can be remedied, which is a keen form of regret.

Two interesting observations follow, by Tennyson and Rossetti, both bearing witness to what could be called the pathology of grief: the way it sharpens perceptions of the world outside.

Poe wails (beautifully), Ralegh's lament and affirmation could not be left out. The laments of Emily Brontë and Anon lead to the more formal kind of lament, both taken from the Irish. 'The Lament for Art O'Leary', from which an extract is taken, is filled with pictures, traditional and intimate at the same time.

John Clare brings us back to what most of us would privately wish for, who have no claim to public lamentation, and Whitman does that service for the unsung heroes.

William Allingham forbids mourning (which instruction, for those left behind, can be a greater cause of trouble than a demand for a full Requiem), and Chesterton rejects such selfish modesty – 'The only way to make less of death is to make more of it.'

Johnson brings hearty common sense to dispose of the matter and that concludes the book.

Not quite; as a cook deserves a tit-bit an editor can be allowed a postscript. Ruminations, exhortations, visions, instructions, howls, humours – the row humanity makes when reflecting on its fate also contains contradictions, as well as consolations. Unamuno sees this as a virtue. Finally Philip Toynbee, in a journal-entry made during his last illness, is diffident and careful as any modern must be, but realistic and hopeful, is dying as he sums up.

Adieu, farewell, earth's bliss,
This world uncertain is,
Fond are life's lustful joys,
Death proves them all but toys,
None from his darts can fly.
I am sick, I must die.
        Lord have mercy on us!

Rich men, trust not in wealth,
Gold cannot buy you health;
Physic himself must fade,
All things to end are made.
The plague full swift goes by;
I am sick, I must die.
        Lord have mercy on us!

Beauty is but a flower
Which wrinkles will devour;
Brightness falls from the air,
Queens have died young and fair,
Dust hath closed Helen's eye.
I am sick, I must die.
        Lord have mercy on us!

Strength stoops unto the grave,
Worms feed on Hector brave,
Swords may not fight with fate,
Earth still holds ope her gate.
'Come! come!' the bells do cry.
I am sick, I must die.
        Lord have mercy on us!

Wit with his wantonness
Tasteth death's bitterness;
Hell's executioner
Hath no ears for to hear
What vain art can reply.
I am sick, I must die.
      Lord have mercy on us!

Haste, therefore, each degree,
To welcome destiny.
Heaven is our heritage,
Earth but a player's stage;
Mount we unto the sky.
I am sick, I must die.
      Lord have mercy on us!

THOMAS NASHE (1567–1601)

So, we'll go no more a-roving
  So late into the night,
Though the heart be still as loving,
  And the moon be still as bright.

For the sword outwears its sheath,
  And the soul wears out the breast,
And the heart must pause to breathe,
  And Love itself have rest.

Though the night was made for loving,
  And the day returns too soon,
Yet we'll go no more a-roving
  By the light of the moon.

LORD BYRON (1788–1824)

When the lamp is shattered,
The light in the dust lies dead;
   When the cloud is scattered,
The rainbow's glory is shed;
   When the lute is broken,
Sweet tones are remembered not;
   When the lips have spoken,
Loved accents are soon forgot.

   As music and splendour
Survive not the lamp and the lute,
   The heart's echoes render
No song when the spirit is mute:–
   No song but sad dirges,
Like the wind through a ruined cell,
   Or the mournful surges
That ring the dead seaman's knell.

   When hearts have once mingled,
Love first leaves the well-built nest;
   The weak one is singled
To endure what it once possessed.
   O Love! who bewailest
The frailty of all things here,
   Why choose you the frailest
For your cradle, your home, and your bier?

   Its passions will rock thee,
As the storms rock the ravens on high;
   Bright reason will mock thee,
Like the sun from a wintry sky.
   From thy nest every rafter
Will rot, and thine eagle home
   Leave thee naked to laughter,
When leaves fall and cold winds come.

P. B. SHELLEY (1792–1822)

To have known him, to have loved him
   After loneness long;
And then to be estranged in life,
   And neither in the wrong;
And now for death to set his seal –
   Ease me, a little ease, my song!

By wintry hills his hermit-mound
   The sheeted snow-drifts drape,
And houseless there the snow-bird flits
   Beneath the fir-trees' crape:
Glazed now with ice the cloistral vine
   That hid the shyest grape.

          HERMAN MELVILLE (1819–91), 'Monody'

Strange, that the mind, when fraught
With a passion so intense
One would think that it well
Might drown all life in the eye –
That it should, by being so overwrought,
Suddenly strike on a sharper sense
For a shell, or a flower, little things
Which else would have been passed by!

          ALFRED TENNYSON (1809–92), from 'Maud'

The wind flapped loose, the wind was still,
Shaken out dead from tree and hill:
I had walked on at the wind's will –
I sat now, for the wind was still.

Between my knees my forehead was –
My lips, drawn in, said not Alas!
My hair was over in the grass,
My naked ears heard the day pass.

My eyes, wide open, had the run
Of some ten weeds to fix upon;

Among those few, out of the sun,
The woodspurge flowered, three cups in one.

From perfect grief there need not be
Wisdom or even memory:
One thing then learnt remains to me –
The woodspurge has a cup of three.

DANTE GABRIEL ROSSETTI (1828–82), 'The Woodspurge'

Thou wast that all to me, love,
    For which my soul did pine –
A green isle in the sea, love,
    A fountain and a shrine,
All wreathed with fairy fruits and flowers,
    And all the flowers were mine.

Ah, dream too bright to last!
    Ah, starry Hope! that didst arise
But to be overcast!
    A voice from out the Future cries,
'On! on!' – but o'er the Past
    (Dim gulf!) my spirit hovering lies
Mute, motionless, aghast!

For, alas! alas! with me
    The light of Life is o'er!
    'No more – no more – no more –'
(Such language holds the solemn sea
    To the sands upon the shore)
Shall bloom the thunder-blasted tree,
    Or the stricken eagle soar!

And all my days are trances,
    And all my nightly dreams
Are where thy dark eye glances,
    And where thy footstep gleams –
In what ethereal dances,
    By what eternal streams.

EDGAR ALLAN POE (1809–49), 'To One in Paradise'

Cold in the earth, and the deep snow piled above thee!
Far, far removed, cold in the dreary grave!
Have I forgot, my Only Love, to love thee,
Severed at last by Time's all-wearing wave?

Now, when alone, do my thoughts no longer hover
Over the mountains on Angora's shore;
Resting their wings where heath and fern-leaves cover
That noble heart for ever, ever more?

Cold in the earth, and fifteen wild Decembers
From those brown hills have melted into spring –
Faithful indeed is the spirit that remembers
After such years of change and suffering!

Sweet Love of youth, forgive if I forget thee
While the world's tide is bearing me along:
Sterner desires and darker hopes beset me,
Hopes which obscure but cannot do thee wrong.

No other Sun has lightened up my heaven;
No other Star has ever shone for me:
All my life's bliss from thy dear life was given –
All my life's bliss is in the grave with thee.

But when the days of golden dreams had perished
And even Despair was powerless to destroy,
Then did I learn how existence could be cherished,
Strengthened and fed without the aid of joy;

Then did I check the tears of useless passion,
Weaned my young soul from yearning after thine;
Sternly denied its burning wish to hasten
Down to that tomb already more than mine!

And even yet, I dare not let it languish,
Dare not indulge in memory's rapturous pain;
Once drinking deep of that divinest anguish,
How could I seek the empty world again?

EMILY BRONTË (1818–48), 'Remembrance'

As you came from the holy land
      Of Walsingham
Met you not with my true love
      By the way as you came?

How shall I know your true love
      That have met many one,
As I went to the holy land
      That have come, that have gone?

She is neither white nor brown
      But as the heavens fair,
There is none hath a form so divine
      In the earth or the air.

Such an one did I meet, good sir,
      Such an angelic face,
Who like a queen, like a nymph, did appear
      By her gait, by her grace.

She hath left me here all alone,
      All alone as unknown,
Who sometimes did me lead with herself,
      And me loved as her own.

What's the cause that she leaves you alone
      And a new way doth take,
Who loved you once as her own
      And her joy did you make?

I have loved her all my youth,
      But now old, as you see;
Love likes not the falling fruit
      From the withered tree.

Know that love is a careless child
      And forgets promise past,
He is blind, he is deaf when he list,
      And in faith never fast.

His desire is a dureless content
    And a trustless joy,
He is won with a world of despair
    And is lost with a toy.

Of women kind such indeed is the love,
    Or the word Love abused,
Under which many childish desires
    And conceits are excused.

But true love is a durable fire,
    In the mind ever burning,
Never sick, never old, never dead,
    From itself never turning.

SIR WALTER RALEGH (1552–1618)

The wind doth blow today, my love,
    And a few small drops of rain.
I never had but one true-love,
    In cold grave she was lain.

I'll do as much for my true-love
    As any young man may,
I'll sit and mourn all at her grave
    For a twelvemonth and a day.

The twelvemonth and a day being up,
    The dead began to speak:
Oh who sits weeping on my grave,
    And will not let me sleep?

'Tis I, my love, sits on your grave,
    And will not let you sleep,
For I crave one kiss of your clay-cold lips,
    And that is all I seek.

You crave one kiss of my clay-cold lips,
    But my breath smells earthy strong.

If you have one kiss of my clay-cold lips,
    Your time will not be long.

'Tis down in yonder garden green,
    Love, where we used to walk,
The finest flower that ere was seen
    Is withered to a stalk.

The stalk is withered dry, my love,
    So will our hearts decay.
So make yourself content, my love,
    Till God calls you away.

        ANON. (traditional), 'The Unquiet Grave'

In a quiet watered land, a land of roses,
    Stands Saint Kieran's city fair;
And the warriors of Erin in their famous generations
    Slumber there.

There beneath the dewy hillside sleep the noblest
    Of the clan of Conn,
Each below his stone with name in branching ogham
    And the sacred knot thereon.

There they laid to rest the seven Kings of Tara,
    There the sons of Cairbrè sleep –
Battle-banners of the Gael that in Kieran's plain of crosses
    Now their final hosting keep.

And in Clonmacnoise they laid the men of Teffia,
    And right many a lord of Breagh;
Deep the sod above Clan Creidè and Clan Conaill,
    Kind in hall and fierce in fray.

Many and many a son of Conn the Hundred-fighter
    In the red earth lies at rest;
Many a blue eye of Clan Colman the turf covers,
    Many a swan-white breast.

    T. W. ROLLESTON (1857–1920), 'Clonmacnoise' (from the Irish)

. . . Could my calls but wake my kindred
In Derrynane beyond the mountains,
Or Capling of the yellow apples,
Many a proud and stately rider,
Many a girl with spotless kerchief,
Would be here before tomorrow,
Shedding tears about your body,
Art O'Leary, once so merry.

My love and my secret,
Your corn is stacked,
Your cows are milking;
On me is the grief
There's no cure for in Munster.
Till Art O'Leary rise
This grief will never yield
That's bruising all my heart
Yet shut up fast in it,
As 'twere in a locked trunk
With the key gone astray,
And rust grown on the wards . . .

EILEEN O'LEARY,
from 'Lament for Art O'Leary' (1773), tr. Frank O'Connor

In midnight sleep of many a face of anguish,
Of the look at first of the mortally wounded (of that
  indescribable look),
Of the dead on their backs with arms extended wide,
    I dream, I dream, I dream.

Of scenes of Nature, fields and mountains,
Of skies so beauteous after a storm, and at night the moon
  so unearthly bright,
Shining sweetly, shining down, where we dig the trenches
  and gather the heaps,
    I dream, I dream, I dream.

Long have they passed, faces and trenches and fields,
Where through the carnage I moved with a callous
    composure, or away from the fallen,
Onward I sped at the time – but now of their forms at night
    I dream, I dream, I dream.

              WALT WHITMAN (1819–92), 'Old War-Dreams'

And David lamented with this lamentation over Saul and over Jonathan
his son.
'The beauty of Israel is slain upon thy high places:
How are the mighty fallen!
Tell it not in Gath,
Publish it not in the streets of Askelon;
Lest the daughters of the Philistines rejoice,
Lest the daughters of the uncircumcised triumph.

Ye mountains of Gilboa,
Let there be no dew, neither let there be rain, upon you,
    nor fields of offerings:
For there the shield of the mighty is vilely cast away,
The shield of Saul, as though he had not been anointed with
    oil.
From the blood of the slain, from the fat of the mighty,
The bow of Jonathan turned not back,
And the sword of Saul returned not empty.
Saul and Jonathan were lovely and pleasant in their lives,
And in their death they were not divided:
They were swifter than eagles,
They were stronger than lions.
Ye daughters of Israel, weep over Saul,
Who clothed you in scarlet, with other delights,
Who put ornaments of gold upon your apparel.
How are the mighty fallen in the midst of the battle!
O Jonathan, thou wast slain in thine high places.
I am distressed for thee, my brother Jonathan:
Very pleasant hast thou been unto me:
Thy love to me was wonderful,

Passing the love of women.
How are the mighty fallen,
And the weapons of war perished!'

II Samuel, chapter 1

And the king said unto Cushi, 'Is the young man Absalom safe?'

And Cushi answered, 'The enemies of my lord the king, and all that rise against thee to do thee hurt, be as that young man is.'

And the king was much moved, and went up to the chamber over the gate, and wept: and as he went, thus he said,

'O my son Absalom, my son, my son Absalom! would God I had died for thee, O Absalom, my son, my son!'

II Samuel, chapter 18

ANTONY: The miserable change now at my end
   Lament nor sorrow at: but please your thoughts
   In feeding them with those my former fortunes
   Wherein I lived: the greatest prince o' the world,
   The noblest; and do now not basely die,
   Not cowardly put off my helmet to
   My countryman: a Roman, by a Roman
   Valiantly vanquished. Now my spirit is going,
   I can no more.
CLEOPATRA: Noblest of men, woo't die?
   Hast thou no care of me, shall I abide
   In this dull world, which in thy absence is
   No better than a sty? O, see, my women:
   The crown o' the earth doth melt.
                             My lord?
O, withered is the garland of the war,
The soldier's pole is fallen: young boys and girls
Are level now with men: the odds is gone,
And there is nothing left remarkable
Beneath the visiting moon.

WILLIAM SHAKESPEARE (1564–1616), *Antony and Cleopatra*

So when sir Bors and his fellows came to his bed they found him stark dead; and he lay as he had smiled, and the sweetest savour about him that ever they felt. Then was there weeping and wringing of hands, and the greatest dole they made that ever made men.

And on the morn the Bishop did his mass of Requiem, and after the Bishop and all the nine knights put sir Launcelot in the same horse-bier that queen Guinevere was laid in before that she was buried. And so the Bishop and they all together went with the body of sir Launcelot daily, till they came to Joyous Garde; and ever they had an hundred torches burning about him.

And so within fifteen days they came to Joyous Garde. And there they laid his corpse in the body of the choir, and sang and read many psalters and prayers over him and about him. And ever his visage was laid open and naked, that all folks might behold him; for such was the custom in those days, that all men of worship should so lie with open visage till that they were buried.

And right thus as they were at their service, there came sir Ector de Maris that had seven years sought all England, Scotland and Wales, seeking his brother, sir Launcelot. And when sir Ector heard such noise and light in the choir of Joyous Garde, he alighted and put his horse from him and came into the choir. And there he saw men sing and weep, and all they knew sir Ector, but he knew not them.

Then went sir Bors unto sir Ector and told him how there lay his brother, sir Launcelot, dead. And then sir Ector threw his shield, sword and helm from him, and when he beheld sir Launcelot's visage he fell down in a swoon. And when he waked it were hard any tongue to tell the doleful complaints that he made for his brother.

'Ah, Launcelot!' he said, 'thou were head of all Christian knights! And now I dare say,' said sir Ector, 'thou sir Launcelot, there thou liest, that thou were never matched of earthly knight's hand. And thou were the courtest knight that ever bare shield! And thou were the truest friend to thy lover that ever bestrode horse, and thou were the truest lover, of a sinful man, that ever loved woman, and thou were the kindest man that ever struck with sword. And thou were the goodliest person that ever came among press of knights, and thou were the meekest man and the gentlest that ever ate in hall among ladies, and thou were the sternest knight to thy mortal foe that ever put spear in the rest.'

Then there was weeping and dolour out of measure.

Thus they kept sir Launcelot's corpse aloft fifteen days, and then they buried it with great devotion. And then at leisure they went all with the Bishop of Canterbury to his hermitage, and there they were together more than a month.

SIR THOMAS MALORY (1471), *Le Morte d'Arthur*

Let us now praise famous men,
And our fathers that begat us.
The Lord hath wrought great glory by them
Through his great power from the beginning.
Such as did bear rule in their kingdoms,
Men renowned for their power,
Giving counsel by their understanding,
And declaring prophecies:
Leaders of the people by their counsels,
And by their knowledge of learning meet for the people,
Wise and eloquent in their instructions:
Such as found out musical tunes,
And recited verses in writing:
Rich men furnished with ability,
Living peaceably in their habitations:
All these were honoured in their generations,
And were the glory of their times.
There be of them, that have left a name behind them,
That their praises might be reported.
And some there be, which have no memorial;
Who are perished, as though they had never been;
And are become as though they had never been born;
And their children after them.
But these were merciful men,
Whose righteousness hath not been forgotten.

Ecclesiasticus (*c*.180 BC)

I would not that my being all should die
    And pass away with every common lot;
I would not that my humble dust should lie
    In quite a strange and unfrequented spot,
    By all unheeded and by all forgot,
With nothing save the heedless winds to sigh,
    And nothing but the dewy morn to weep
About my grave, far hid from the world's eye:
I fain would have some friend to wander nigh,
    And find a path to where my ashes sleep –
Not the cold heart that merely passes by
    To read who lies beneath, but such as keep
Past memories warm with deeds of other years,
And pay to Friendship some few friendly tears.

           JOHN CLARE (1793–1864), 'Memory'

With music strong I come, with my cornets and my drums,
I play not marches for accepted victors only, I play marches
    for conquered and slain persons.

Have you heard that it was good to gain the day?
I also say it is good to fall, battles are lost in the same spirit
    in which they are won.
I beat and pound for the dead,
I blow through my embouchures my loudest and gayest for
    them.

Vivas to those who have failed!
And to those whose war-vessels sank in the sea!
And to those themselves who sank in the sea!
And to all generals that lost engagements, and all overcome
    heroes!
And the numberless unknown heroes equal to the greatest
    heroes known!

           WALT WHITMAN, from 'Song of Myself'

No funeral gloom, my dears, when I am gone,
Corpse-gazing tears, black raiment, graveyard grimness;
Think of me as withdrawn into the dimness,
Yours still, you mine; remember all the best
Of our past moments, and forget the rest;
   And so, to where I wait, come gently on.

WILLIAM ALLINGHAM (1824–89)

The very poor are always despised and rebuked because of their fuss and expenditure on funerals. Only to-day I saw that a public body refused aid to those who had gone any length in such expenditure. Now I do not mean that their crape is my abstract conception of robes of mourning, or that the conversation of Mrs Brown with Mrs Jones over the coffin has the dignity of 'Lycidas'. I do not even say that educated people could not do it better. I say that they are not trying to do it at all. Educated people have got some chilly fad to the effect that making a fuss about death is morbid or vulgar. The educated people are entirely wrong on the fundamental point of human psychology. The uneducated people are entirely right on the point.

The one way to make bereavement tolerable is to make it important. To gather your friends, to have a gloomy festival, to talk, to cry, to praise the dead – all that does change the atmosphere, and carry human nature over the open grave. The nameless torture is to try and treat it as something private and casual, as our elegant stoics do. That is at once pride and pain and hypocrisy. The only way to make less of death is to make more of it.

G. K. CHESTERTON (1874–1936)

On my dear grandchild Simon Bradstreet, who died on
16th November 1669, being but a month and one day old
No sooner come, but gone, and fallen asleep,
Acquaintance short, yet parting caused us weep.
Three flowers, two scarcely blown, the last i' the bud,
Cropped by the Almighty's hand; yet he is good.

With dreadful awe before him let's be mute;
Such was his will, but why, let's not dispute;
With humble hearts and mouths put in the dust,
Let's say he's merciful as well as just.
He will return, and make up all our losses,
And smile again, after our bitter crosses.
Go pretty babe, go rest with sisters twain,
Among the blest in endless joys remain.

ANNE BRADSTREET (*c.*1612–72)

An epitaph upon a young married couple
dead and buried together
To these, whom death again did wed,
This grave's their second marriage-bed.
For though the hand of Fate could force
'Twixt soul and body a divorce,
It could not sunder man and wife,
'Cause they both livéd but one life.
Peace, good reader. Do not weep.
Peace, the lovers are asleep.
They, sweet turtles, folded lie
In the last knot love could tie.
And though they lie as they were dead,
Their pillow stone, their sheets of lead
(Pillow hard, and sheets not warm),
Love made the bed; they'll take no harm.
Let them sleep, let them sleep on,
Till this stormy night be gone,
Till th' eternal morrow dawn;
Then the curtains will be drawn
And they wake into a light
Whose day shall never die in night.

RICHARD CRASHAW (1613–49)

As waked from sleep, methought I heard the voice
Of one that mourned; I listened to the noise.
I looked, and quickly found it was my dear;
Dead as she was, I little thought her there.
I questioned her with tenderness, while she
Sighed only, but would else still silent be.
I waked indeed; the lovely mourner's gone,
She sighs no more, 'tis I that sigh alone.

Musing on her, I slept again, but where
I went I know not, but I found her there.
Her lovely eyes she kindly fixed on me,
'Let Miser not be nangry then,' said she,
A language love had taught, and love alone
Could teach; we prattled as we oft had done,
But she, I know not how, was quickly gone.

With her imaginary presence blessed,
My slumbers are emphatically rest;
I of my waking thoughts can little boast,
They always sadly tell me she is lost.
Much of our happiness we always owe
To error, better to believe than know!
Return, delusion sweet, and oft return!
I joy, mistaken; undeceived, I mourn;
But all my sighs and griefs are fully paid,
When I but see the shadow of her shade.

JONATHAN RICHARDSON (1667–1745), 'On My Dreaming of My Wife'

Getting over it so soon? But the words are ambiguous. To say
the patient is getting over it after an operation for appendicitis
is one thing; after he's had his leg off it is quite another. After
that operation either the wounded stump heals or the man dies.
If it heals, the fierce, continuous pain will stop. Presently he'll
get back his strength and be able to stump about on his wooden
leg. He has 'got over it'. But he will probably have recurrent
pains in the stump all his life, and perhaps pretty bad ones; and
he will always be a one-legged man.

C. S. LEWIS (1898–1963), *A Grief Observed*

Sorrow is a kind of rust of the soul, which every new idea contributes in its passage to scour away. It is the putrefaction of stagnant life, and is remedied by exercise and motion.

SAMUEL JOHNSON (1709–84)

*   *   *   *   *   *   *   *   *

Several times in the devious course of these essays I have defined, in spite of my horror of definitions, my own position with regard to the problem that I have been examining; but I know there will always be some dissatisfied reader, educated in some dogmatism or other, who will say: 'This man comes to no conclusion, he vacillates – now he seems to affirm one thing and then its contrary – he is full of contradictions – I can't label him. What is he?' Just this – one who affirms contraries, a man of contradiction and strife, as Jeremiah said of himself; one who says one thing with his heart and the contrary with his head, and for whom this conflict is the very stuff of life. And that is as clear as the water that flows from the melted snow upon the mountain tops.

I shall be told that this is an untenable position, that a foundation must be laid upon which to build our action and our works, that it is impossible to live by contradictions, that unity and clarity are essential conditions of life and thought, and that it is necessary to unify thought. And this leaves us as we were before. For it is precisely this inner contradiction that unifies my life and gives it its practical purpose.

Or rather it is the conflict itself, it is this self-same passionate uncertainty, that unifies my action and makes me live and work.

MIGUEL DE UNAMUNO (1864–1936), *The Tragic Sense of Life*

Sudden wild nostalgia for my very earliest, cloudiest Communist days; the pamphlet John Cornford sent me at Rugby, a black silhouette of Lenin with arm outstretched against a field of deep maroon; the Parton Street bookshop; my first meeting of the October Club at Oxford . . . How clearly it all comes back to me now, those passionate longings for brotherhood with the whole world and the conviction that my own emancipation, freedom, growth were directly dependent on working for that glorious fraternity. What worlds unfolding! What wild and confident happiness!

Never for a moment have I felt this kind of ecstasy from any of my religious aspirations. And although it is true, of course, that Communism was a god that failed, the *hope* was real enough. Bliss was it in that dawn to be alive – however false the dawn.

And now I feel again the ancient, visionary hope, as my body aches, rumbles and belches, of the freed soul winging away from this gross prison and joining all the company of heaven.

Is this just as great an illusion as the others? Well, it has better credentials at least.

PHILIP TOYNBEE (1916–81), *End of a Journey*

Notes

Dates in brackets are dates of first publication or of a later edition used as a source; 'wr.' indicates date of writing, when known. Spelling has been modernized throughout; other modernization noted.

Love

pp 3 –16

MILTON, *Paradise Lost* (1667), Book 4, lines 321–55.

C. BRONTË, *Jane Eyre* (1848), chapter 38.

KEATS, letter 24 February (1820 (?)). No. 188 in *The Letters of John Keats*, ed. Forman (1947).

CLARE, wr. 1842–62, 1st pub. in *Later Poems*, ed. Robinson and Powell (1984).

DANTE, *La Vita Nuova* (The New Life), part XI (wr. 1290–94); tr. William Anderson (1964).

DONNE, *Songs and Sonnets* (1633).

SHAKESPEARE, Sonnet 116.

LANDOR, *Works* (1846).

BURNS, *Johnson's 'Scots Musical Museum' 1788–1803*. Spelling englished.

SHAKESPEARE, *Much Ado About Nothing* (wr. *c.*1598), act 2, scene 3.

SUCKLING, song from *Aglaura* (1638).

WHITMAN, *Leaves of Grass* (1891 edition), from 'Calamus' section.

SPENSER, *Amoretti* (1595), Sonnet 68.

LEWIS, *A Grief Observed* (1961), from part 3.

WEIL, *Waiting on God* (*Attente de Dieu*), tr. Emma Craufurd (1951), p.77, 'The Love of God and Affliction'.

Christianity

VILLON, *'Ballade pour prier Notre-Dame'* from *Le Grand Testament*, tr. LOWELL, *Imitations* (1962 edn.).

ANON (16th-century Spanish), *'A Cristo Crucificado'*, tr. C. E. Ward.

BLAKE, *Jerusalem* (wr. and etched 1804–20), chapter 4, from part 96.

DONNE, *The Divine Poems*, ed. Gardner (1952).

VAUGHAN, *Silex Scintillans* (1655).

CHESTERTON, from 'The Flag of the World', in *Orthodoxy* (1908).

TRAHERNE, 'The First Century', no. 46. *Centuries, Poems and Thanksgivings*, ed. Margoliouth (1958).

HOPKINS, 'God's Grandeur' (wr. 1877).

JULIAN, *Revelations of Divine Love*, chapter 5, 'The First Revelation', version 'from the MS in the British Museum' by Grace Warrack (1901), with some further modernization.

LAW, no. 15 in Geoffrey Grigson's anthology *The Romantics* (1942). His note: 'from a letter to Thomas Yate, 1756, quoted in Walton's "Notes and Materials for an Adequate Biography of William Law" (1854)'.

WISDOM OF SOLOMON, chapter 11, verses 21–26, Authorized Version of the Bible (1611), Apocrypha. This book is part of the canon in R.C. bibles.

ABELARD, from letter 4, *The Letters of Abelard and Heloise*, tr. Betty Radice (1974).

DANTE, *La Divina Commedia* (wr. *c*.1300), *Paradiso*, canto 3, lines 64–90 (the First Circle), tr. C. E. Ward.

COWPER, *Olney Hymns* (1779).

TOYNBEE, *End of a Journey, an autobiographical journal 1979–81*, ed. Bullimore (1988). Quoting from Søren Kierkegaard (1813–55), *Journals*, ed. Dru (1938), and Abbé de Tourville, *Letters of Direction*, ed. Dacre Press (1939).

DONNE, 'A Litanie', verses 15–17. *Divine Poems*, ed. Gardner (1952).

ROPER, *Life* of his father-in-law Sir (St.) Thomas More (1626).

JULIAN, *Revelations of Divine Love*, chapter 27, 'The Thirteenth Revelation', version by Grace Warrack (1901) with some further modernization.

HERBERT, *The Temple* (1633), from 'The Church' group. *Works*, ed. Hutchinson (1941).

PASCAL, *Pensées* (1670), no. 391, tr. J. M. Cohen (1961).

TOYNBEE, *Part of a Journey, an autobiographical journal 1977–79* (1981).

MORE, *Treatise on the Passion* (Christ answering us). Wr. (unfinished) in prison, part in English, part in Latin, tr. his grand-daughter Mary Basset.

MOLTKE, letter to his wife, 10 January 1945, before his execution. From *Dying We Live* (tr. Kahn, 1956) in *The Protestant Mystics*, ed. Fremantle and Auden (1964). (Also in *Letters to Freya, 1939–45*, tr. & ed. von Oppen, 1991.)

RALEGH, 'Even such is time', a verse from an earlier love poem, with last lines said to have been added before his execution. *Selected Writings*, ed. Hammond (1984).

AUGUSTINE, *Confessions*, Book 9, from parts 14, 29 and 30, tr. Pine-Coffin (1961).

MILTON, Sonnet 16 (wr. ?1652). Compare 'To Mr Cyriack Skinner' in the 'Human Solidarity' section (p.65).

HERBERT, *The Temple* (1633).

WILDE, *De Profundis* (1905), a letter to Lord Alfred Douglas wr. from prison, 1898.

MUIR, *Collected Poems* (1952).

WEIL, *Notebooks* (*Cahiers*), vol. I, tr. Wills (1956), p.304.

AUDEN, from his introduction to *The Protestant Mystics*, ed. Fremantle and Auden (1964).

NEWMAN, *Apologia Pro Vita Sua* (1864).

J. C. POWYS, *Autobiography* (1934), chapter 12.

PASCAL, *Pensées* (1670), no. 830, tr. J. M. Cohen (1961).

Human Solidarity

YEATS, *The Winding Stair* (1933).

POPE, *An Essay on Man* (1733–4), Epistle 2, lines 1–18.

SCHOPENHAUER, *MS Remains* vol. 4, *MS Books* 1830–52, tr. Payne, ed. Hubscher (1988–90).

WHITMAN, *Leaves of Grass* (1891 edition), 'Song of Myself' (1st pub. 1855), lines 1278–81.

TRAHERNE, from 'The Fourth Century', no. 55. *Centuries, Poems and Thanksgivings*, ed. Margoliouth (1958).

SWIFT, *Thoughts on Various Subjects*, no. 25 (1727), from a miscellany compiled with Pope. *Selected Writings*, ed. Hayward (1946).

COLERIDGE, *The Notebooks of Samuel Taylor Coleridge*, vol. II, no. 2210, ed. Coburn (1961).

MARCUS AURELIUS, *Meditations*, Book 12, no. 6, tr. Staniforth (1964).

SCOTT, *Journals*, ed. Anderson (1972).

KEATS, no. 98 in *Letters*, ed. Forman (1947).

RILKE, *Poems*, tr. Leishman (1966). Original (1913) version of the 10th Duino Elegy.

SMITH, *Letters*, ed. Nowell C. Smith (1956).

COWPER, *Memoirs of the early life of William Cowper, written by himself* (1816). Quoted in the introduction by F. E. Hutchinson to *Works of George Herbert* (1941).

SMETHAM, *Literary Works*, ed. Davies (1893). No. 60 in Grigson's *The Victorians* (1950).

FORSTER, *Commonplace Book*, ed. Gardner (1985).

KEATS, from a letter to Benjamin Bailey, Nov. 1817; no. 31 in *Letters*, ed. Forman (1947).

RUSKIN, *Modern Painters*, vol. III, part 4, chapter ix, nos. 14 and 15. No. 92 in Kenneth Clark's *Ruskin Today* (1964).

GOETHE; Johann Eckermann, *Conversations with Goethe* (in 1825).

SCHOPENHAUER, *MS Remains*, tr. Payne (1988), vol. I, *Early MSS* (1814); no. 131.

MONTAIGNE, *Essays*, Book II, tr. J. M. Cohen (1958).

SOUTHWELL, *Poets of the English Language*, vol. II, ed. Auden and Pearson (1952).

KEATS, from a letter to Charles Brown, Sept. 1819; no. 155 in *Letters*, ed. Forman (1947).

JOHNSON, *The Rambler*, 1750, vol. II, no. 29.

BOSWELL, letter dated August 1775 in *Life of Samuel Johnson* (1791).

CHAUCER, 'Le Bon Conseil de G. Chaucer', 3rd verse, modernized. Also called 'Truth' and 'Balade de Bon Conseyl'.

SCOVELL, *Collected Poems* (1988).

VAN GOGH, from a letter to his brother Theo, July 1883, written from The Hague. *The Letters of Vincent Van Gogh*, ed. Roskill (1963).

POPE, *An Essay on Man* (1733–34), Epistle II, part 4.

HERNÁNDEZ, *El Gaucho Martín Fierro* (1872–9), part 2 ('The Return'), canto 30, tr. C. E. Ward (1967).

SENECA, *On Providence* IV, 9–10, tr. Basore (1928).

SCHOPENHAUER, *MS Remains*, tr. Payne (1988), vol. I, *Early MSS*, Weimar 1814.

BOETHIUS, *Consolations of Philosophy*, Book II, part vii, tr. Watts (1969).

KEATS, from a letter to his brother, Feb–May 1819; no. 123 in *Letters*, ed. Forman (1947).

FREUD, *Analysis Terminable and Interminable* (1937), tr. and quoted by Bruno Bettelheim in *Freud and Man's Soul* (1982).

BACON, *Essays* (various editions pub. 1597–1625).

PEACOCK, *Nightmare Abbey* (1818), from chapter 7.

CHESTERTON, from 'What Is Right with the World', *T.P.'s Weekly* (1910). In *The Bodley Head G. K. Chesterton*, ed. P. J. Kavanagh (1985).

GRIGSON, from 'Poems and Pleasures' in *Blessings, Kicks and Curses, A Critical Collection* (1982).

GOETHE; Johann Eckermann, *Conversations with Goethe* (in 1828).

SMITH, letter to Francis Jeffrey, 1804, in *Letters*, ed. Nowell C. Smith (1956).

BELLOW, *Herzog* (1964), chapter 3.

MACNEICE, *Collected Poems*, 1957–60 section, ed. Dodds (1966).

YEATS, part 2 of 'A Dialogue of Self and Soul', *The Winding Stair and Other Poems* (1933).

MILLER, *The Colossus of Maroussi* (1941), from part 2. On Phaestos, Crete.

BRODSKY, from 'To Urania', tr. Brodsky; *Selected Poems 1965–85* (1988).

WHITMAN, *Leaves of Grass* (1891 edition), 'Song of Myself' (1st pub. 1855), lines 822–9.

JONSON, 'To the Immortall Memorie . . .', lines 43–74; *Underwoods*, LXX. *Complete Poems*, ed. Parfitt (1975). The poem's divisions imitate those of Pindar's odes.

MILTON, Sonnet 18, known as 'To Mr Cyriack Skinner Upon His Blindness' (wr. ?1655). Compare the earlier sonnet in the 'Christianity' section (p.31).

MONTAIGNE, *Essays*, Book III, tr. J. M. Cohen (1958), from chapter 12.

BURNS, 'For A' That' (1800). *Poems*, ed. Meikle and Beattie (1946).

WORDSWORTH, 'Resolution and Independence' (1807), verses 15–20 (end).

JOHNSON, *The Rambler*, 1750, no. 68.

CHESTERTON, from 'On the Institution of the Family', in *Heretics* (1905).

HOPKINS, 'Brothers' (wr. 1879).

PRIOR, 'Jinny the Just', lines 43–96. (Wr. by 1708, pub. 1908.)

R. S. THOMAS, *Selected Poems 1946–68*.

P. J. KAVANAGH, *Presences* (1987).

GURNEY, 'The Escape' (wr. 1919–22); *Collected Poems*, ed. P. J. Kavanagh (1982).

PATRICK KAVANAGH, 'The Hospital' (1956); *Complete Poems* (Ireland, 1984).

Personal Faith

SWIFT, 'Thoughts on Religion' (1765). *Selected Writings*, ed. Hayward (1946).

POPE, from a letter to Richard Steele, July 1712. No. 165 in Grigson's *Before the Romantics* (1946), 1984 edn.

CICERO, *De Senectute* (On Old Age), tr. Grant; *Selected Works* (1960).

PLATO, *The Apology of Socrates*, tr. Tredennick. *The Last Days of Socrates* (1954). Socrates (469–399 BC) was condemned to death for heresy and 'corrupting the minds of the young'.

BOSWELL, *Life of Samuel Johnson* (1791), year 1772.

DONNE, from a sermon preached at Whitehall, 1622. *Selected Prose*, ed. Rhodes (1987).

WALTON, *Life of Dr John Donne* (1640).

LEWIS, *A Grief Observed* (1961), from part 4.

GOETHE; Johann Eckermann, *Conversations with Goethe* (in 1824).

TOYNBEE, *Part of a Journey, an autobiographical journal 1977–79*, p.395.

HAZLITT, from 'On the Fear of Death' (1822). *Selected Essays*, ed. Keynes (1944).

WILDER, *The Ides of March* (1948), book 3. Julius Caesar at the deathbed of Catullus.

PLATO, *Phaedo*, tr. Tredennick, *The Last Days of Socrates* (1954).

SMITH, in *Letters*, ed. Nowell C. Smith (1956).

PLUTARCH, 'Letter of Consolation to His Wife', parts 1–3. *Moralia (Moral Essays)*, tr. Midgley (1870), with some modernization.

JOHNSON, letter to James Elphinston, 1750, in Boswell's *Life of Samuel Johnson* (1791).

JOHNSON, letter to Mrs Strahan, 1781, in Boswell's *Life* (as above).

BLAKE, letter (1800) to W. Hayley (his patron) on the death of Hayley's son Thomas, aged 20. *Poetry and Prose*, ed. Hayward (1946).

DICKINSON, letter to Miss Maria Whitney, 1879. *The Protestant Mystics*, ed. Fremantle and Auden (1964).

RALEGH, from a letter to Sir Robert Ceil on the death of Cecil's wife, 1597. *Selected Writings*, ed. Hammond (1984).

RALEGH, from a letter to Lady Ralegh on the death of their son Wat, 1618.

HUDSON, *Far Away and Long Ago* (1918), from chapter 30.

UNAMUNO, *The Tragic Sense of Life* (*Del Sentimiento Trágico de la Vida*) (1912), tr. J. E. Crawford Flitch (1954 edn.), from chapter 11, 'The Practical Problem'.

TOYNBEE, *End of a Journey, an autobiographical journal 1979–81* (1981), p.374.

WEIL, *Notebooks*, tr. Wills (1956), p.238.

WILDE, *De Profundis* (1905).

HOPKINS, 'My own heart' (wr. ?1885).

THOMPSON, 'Once in a saintly passion' (wr. 1865). No. 354 in *The New Oxford Book of Victorian Verse*, ed. Ricks (1987).

TRAHERNE, 'Christian Ethicks', V (1675). *Centuries, Poems and Thanksgivings*, ed. Margoliouth (1958).

SMART, *A Song to David* (1763), verses 44–50.

STEVENSON, from 'A Christmas Sermon' (1890).

JULIAN, *Revelations of Divine Love*, 'The Sixteenth Revelation', version by Grace Warrack (1901).

UNAMUNO, *The Tragic Sense of Life* (*Del Sentimiento Trágico de la Vida*)

(1912), tr. Crawford Flitch (1954 edn.); from the final chapter, 'Don Quixote Today'.

MELVILLE, from a letter to Hawthorne, 1851, quoted by E. M. Forster in his *Commonplace Book* (1936). (Melville's *Letters*, ed. Davis and Gilman (1960).)

SHAKESPEARE, *Hamlet* (wr. *c.*1600), act 4, scene 4.

BAUDELAIRE, *Intimate Journals* (*Mon Coeur Mis à Nu*), tr. Chrisopher Isherwood (1930). (1964 edn.)

NIJINSKY, Epilogue to his *Diary* (1918–19), tr. Romola Nijinsky (1st pub. in England 1937).

TENNYSON, from *Morte d'Arthur* (1842). (Lines 407–16 of 'The Passing of Arthur' in *Idylls of the King*, 1869.)

BLAKE, *Jerusalem* (wr. and etched 1804–20), part 10, from chapter 1.

WEIL, *Notebooks*, vol. 2, tr. Wills (1956), pp.471–2.

LAWRENCE, from a letter to Dr Trigant Burrow, August 1927. *The Letters of D. H. Lawrence*, ed. Huxley (1932).

WORDSWORTH, from 'Lines Composed a Few Miles above Tintern Abbey, on Revisiting the Banks of the Wye during a Tour' (1798).

YEATS, *Mythologies* (1962), p.68: *The Celtic Twilight*, 'A Voice' (1902).

BLAKE, *Jerusalem* (wr. and etched 1804–20), chapter 4, from part 98.

WHITMAN, *Leaves of Grass* (1871 edition), 'Chanting the Square Deific', 1st pub. 1865.

R. BROWNING, 'Bishop Blougram's Apology' (1855), lines 163–202.

MORRIS, *News From Nowhere* (1891), from chapter 18, 'The Beginning of the New Life'.

L. POWYS, *Glory of Life* (1934).

ECCLESIASTES, chapter 9, verses 7–10, Authorized Version of the Bible (1611). Revised Version (1898).

WOOLF, from 'A Sketch of the Past' in *Moments of Being, unpublished autobiographical pieces* (1976).

WEIL, *Notebooks*, vol. 2, tr. Wills (1956), p.469.

JUNG, *Alchemical Studies*, commentary on the Chinese text 'T'ai I Chin Hua Tsung Chih' (1968 edn.)

BLAKE, 'Mock On' (wr. *c.*1800–3). *Complete Prose and Poetry*, ed. Keynes (1927). (1989 edn.)

Defiance

EMERSON, 'The Past' from 'Nature and Life' section, *Poems* (1914 edn.).

PATMORE, *'Magnus est Veritas'*, 1877.

YEATS, *Responsibilities* (1914). Said to have been written for Augusta Gregory.

WHITMAN, *Leaves of Grass* (1891 edn.), 'Ah poverties . . .', 1st pub. 1865.

BRONTË, 'Fall Leaves' (wr. 1838). *Poems*, ed. Henderson (1947).

NEWTON, *Memoirs of Sir Isaac Newton*, by Sir David Brewster (1855). No. 83 in Grigson's anthology *Before the Romantics* (1984 edn.).

MILLER, *Tropic of Cancer* (1934). (1965 edn.)

ANON., 'Tom o' Bedlam's Song' (16th–17th century), also called 'Loving Mad Tom'. *Poets of the English Language*, ed. Auden and Pearson, vol. II (1952).

SHAKESPEARE, *Henry IV, Part I* (wr. *c.*1597), act 5, scene 1.

CLARE, 'I Am', wr. in Northampton Asylum, 1844–6.

THOREAU, 'They made me . . .', version in the edition of Thoreau's writings (in progress), University of California Press. *The Oxford Book of Short Poems* (1985).

HENLEY, *'Invictus'* (wr. 1875).

GAY, epitaph on his tomb in Westminster Abbey.

WEBSTER, *The Duchess of Malfi* (wr. 1613), act 5, scene 3.

SHELLEY, 'Ozymandias' (1818).

POE, *Complete Tales and Poems* (1938 edn.).

FITZGERALD, *The Rubáiyát of Omar Khayyám of Naishapur* (1859), verses 78–81 (of later version).

BYRON, *Childe Harold's Pilgrimage* (1816), canto III, stanzas 113–14.

ARNOLD, 'Dover Beach' (1867). Written on his honeymoon.

Comedy

JOB, *The Book of Job*, tr. Stephen Mitchell (San Francisco, 1987), from 'The Summation' and 'The Voice from the Whirlwind'.

LEWIS, *A Grief Observed* (1961), from part 4.

MARCUS AURELIUS, *Meditations*, Book 12, no. 5, tr. Staniforth (1964).

KEILLOR, from 'Laying On Our Backs Looking Up At The Stars', in *We Are Still Married* (1989).

CARROLL, *Through the Looking-Glass and What Alice Found There* (1871), from chapter 6.

PEACOCK, *Nightmare Abbey* (1818), from chapter 5.

CARROLL, *The Hunting of the Snark* (1876), from Fit the Second.

GRAVES, *Collected Poems* (1965).

BOSWELL, *Life of Samuel Johnson* (1791), year 1777.

WHITMAN, *Leaves of Grass* (1891 edn.), 'I Sing the Body Electric' (1st pub. 1855), part 4.

AUSTEN, *Pride and Prejudice* (1813), from chapter 42.

CONNOLLY, *The Unquiet Grave* (1944); p.43 of 1951 edn.

GURNEY, *Collected Poems* (1982).

MONTAIGNE, *Essays*, Book 2, tr. J. M. Cohen (1988), from chapter 17.

MONTAIGNE, as above.

YEATS, *Autobiographies* (1955), 'Reveries over Childhood and Youth', from part 7.

CLOUGH, *Dipsychus* (1865), from scene 4.

PRAED, 'The Season', 9th (last) verse. (*Poems* 1864.)

BYRON, *Don Juan* (1819–24), canto 13, stanzas 3–6.

SWIFT, from 'Verses on the Death of Dr Swift D.S.P.D., by Himself' (wr. 1731). Occasioned by reading a Maxim in Rochefoucauld: (tr.) 'In the Adversity of our best friends, we find something that doth not displease us.' *Selected Writings*, ed. Hayward (1946).

Pleasures

BLAKE, from a letter to Dr Trusler, 1799. *Poetry and Prose*, ed. Keynes (1927).

TRAHERNE, from 'The First Century', no. 36. *Centuries, Poems and Thanksgivings*, ed. Margoliouth (1958).

COLERIDGE, second and third parts of 'This Lime-Tree Bower My Prison' (wr. 1797).

LAMB, from a letter to Wordsworth, January 1801. No. 187 in Grigson's *The Romantics* (1942).

MARCUS AURELIUS, *Meditations*, tr. Staniforth (1964), Book 4, from no. 3.

BROWNING, E. B. 'The Best Thing in the World' (1862).

WHITMAN, *Leaves of Grass* (1891 edn.). 'A Clear Midnight' 1st pub. 1881.

FLETCHER, song from *The Tragedy of Valentinian*, performed 1610–14.

MARVELL, 'The Garden' (wr. *c.*1650), verses 5 and 6.

GRIGSON, *Notes from an Odd Country* (1970), p. 170.

CONNOLLY, *The Unquiet Grave* (1944); p. 64 in the 1951 edn.

NERUDA, *Geografía de Pablo Neruda* (1973), tr. C. E. Ward. On his house at Isla Negra, Chile.

CONNOLLY, *The Unquiet Grave* (1944); p.67 of 1951 edn.

WARD, *The Poetical Entertainer* (1713). No. 42 in *The New Oxford Book of 18th Century Verse*, ed. Lonsdale (1984).

BOSWELL, *Life of Samuel Johnson* (1791), year 1777.

BURNS, 'Green Grow the Rashes' (1787).

MOORE, from chapter 22, *A Story-Teller's Holiday* (1928 edn.)

JONSON, *Underwoods*, II, 'A Celebration of Charis in Ten Lyric Pieces';

NO. 4, 'Her Triumph', verses 2 and 3. *Complete Poems*, ed. Parfitt (1975).

GRIGSON, *Notes from an Odd Country* (1970), p.73. At their house at Troo, Touraine.

WINCHILSEA, 'The Petition for an Absolute Retreat', lines 1–23 and 104–11. *Poems* (1713).

SHAKESPEARE, *As You Like It* (wr. *c.*1597), act 2, scene 1.

BYRON, *Don Juan* (1819–24), canto 13, stanzas 75–7.

CLARE, 'House or window flies' (1st pub. 1920), wr. in Northampton Asylum.

DAVY, from an early notebook, quoted in *Memoirs of the Life of Sir Humphry Davy* by John Davy, 1839. No. 157 in Grigson's *The Romantics* (1942).

MILLER, *The Colossus of Maroussi* (1941).

HOPKINS, 'Inversnaid' (wr. 1881).

JONES, 'High Summer' (1943). No. 127 in *The New Oxford Book of Victorian Verse*, ed. Ricks (1987).

RENTON, 'After Nightfall' (1876). No. 432 in *The New Oxford Book of Victorian Verse* (1987).

CLARE, 'The Lark's Nest' (wr. 1825–30).

COWPER, 'Epitaph on a Hare' (wr. 1783).

COWPER, *The Task* (1785), Book 5, 'The Winter Morning Walk', lines 45–51.

WATSON, *Epigrams* (1884). No. 450 in *The New Oxford Book of Victorian Verse* (1987).

E. THOMAS, 'A Cat' (wr. 1915).

DUFAULT, *On Balance* (1978) (USA).

GURNEY, *Collected Poems* (1982).

KEATS, from a letter to his brother, September 1819. No. 156 in *Letters*, ed. Forman (1947).

PATRICK KAVANAGH, 'Epic' (1951), *Complete Poems* (Ireland, 1984).

RUSKIN, *Mornings in Florence* (1875–7), no. 37, 'The Second Morning'. No. 201 in Kenneth Clark's *Ruskin Today* (1964).

LEOPARDI, *Zibaldone* 259–60, epigraph to *Moral Tales*, tr. Patrick Creagh (1983).

PASTERNAK, from a letter to Olga Friedenberg, 1953, in *The Correspondance of Boris Pasternak and Olga Friedenberg 1910–54*, tr. and ed. Elliott Mossman with Margaret Wettlin (1982).

YEATS, *Mythologies* (1959), *Per Amica Silentia Luna* (1917), 'Anima Mundi', from part 21.

YEATS, *The Winding Stair* (1933), part 4 of 'Vacillation'.

VAN GOGH, from letters to his brother from Arles, August and September 1888. *Letters*, ed. Roskill (1963 edn.)

ARNOLD, from 'The Study of Poetry', in *Essays in Criticism*, 2nd series (1888).

YEATS, *Autobiographies* (1955); *The Trembling of the Veil* (1926), 'Four Years 1887–91', from part 2.

HERBERT, 'The Flower', lines 36–42, *The Temple* (1633).

ARNOLD, from a letter to A. H. Clough, November 1853.

FORSTER, *Commonplace Book*, 'Midnight, 5.9.1936'.

KEATS, from a letter to his brother, September 1819. No. 156 in *Letters*, ed. Forman (1947).

BYRD, Preface to his *Psalms, Sonets, Songs of Sadnes and Pietie* (1588).

BROWNING, 'Abt Vogler', verses 10–12; *Dramatis Personae* (1864).

Age

CASTIGLIONE, *The Book of the Courtier* (1528), beginning of the Second Book, tr. Bull.

BISHOP, 'Epigram' from *Poetical Works* (1796). No. 573 in *The New Oxford Book of 18th Century Verse*, ed. Lonsdale (1984).

PO CHÜ-I, Arthur Waley (1889–1966), *170 Chinese Poems* (1918).

SWIFT, 'Stella's Birthday, March 13th 1727'. She died the next year, aged 42.

JOHNSON, in Boswell's *Life of Samuel Johnson* (1791).

SWIFT, 'Resolutions When I Come To Be Old' (1699).

SWIFT, 'Thoughts on Various Subjects' (1711).

CARROLL, *Through the Looking-Glass* (1871), from chapter 7.

WHITMAN, from the Preface to *Leaves of Grass, Second Annex* (1891) (aged 72).

EMERSON, *Poems* (1865).

LAO TSE (attrib.) (*c.*400 BC), *Tao Te Ching*, no. 47, tr. Lau (1963).

FORSTER, *Commonplace Book* (p.230) in 1961, on J. R. Ackerley (1896–1967).

GRIGSON, *Persephone's Flowers* (1986).

J. C. POWYS, *Autobiography* (1934), from chapter 9, 'Europe'.

PERLÈS, *A Snail's Pace Suits Me Fine* (1973) (aged 76).

YEATS, *Meditations in Time of Civil War*, last verse of part 7, 'I See Phantoms of Hatred and of the Heart's Fullness and of the Coming Emptiness' (wr. 1923, aged 58), in *The Tower* (1928).

CICERO, *De Senectute*, tr. Grant (1960).

FORSTER, *Commonplace Book* (p.231) in 1961 (aged 82).

MOORE, *Irish Melodies* (1807).

ROCHESTER (attrib.), *The Penguin Book of Restoration Verse*, ed. Love (1968).

PEELE (attrib.), 'A Sonet', from *Polyhymnia* (1590).

SHAKESPEARE, Sonnet 78.

HERBERT, *The Temple* (1633).

STEVENSON, 'Requiem' (wr. 1880–4, pub. 1887).

CAMPION, *Bookes of Ayres* (1601–17).

MORRIS, written for an embroidered bed-curtain at 'the old house by the Thames'.

SENECA, from letter 14 in *Letters from a Stoic (Epistulae Morales ad Lucilium)*, tr. Campbell (1969).

BOSWELL, *Life of Samuel Johnson* (1791), year 1784, when Johnson died, aged 75.

Lament

NASHE, song from *Summer's Last Will and Testament* (1600).

BYRON, *Letters and Journals* (1830).

SHELLEY, *Posthumous Poems* (1824).

MELVILLE, *Works*, vol. 16, 1924. *The Oxford Book of Short Poems* (1985).

TENNYSON, *Maud* (1855), from part II, 8.

ROSSETTI, 'The Woodspurge' (wr. 1856).

POE, 'To One In Paradise' (1835).

E. BRONTË, 'Cold in the Earth' (wr. 1845). *Poems*, ed. Henderson (1947).

RALEGH, *Selected Writings*, ed. Hammond (1984).

ANON., 'The Unquiet Grave', 1st pub. 1868, from oral tradition in Sussex.

ROLLESTON, version 'from the Irish of Angus O'Gillan'.

O'LEARY, from 'The Lament for Art O'Leary' (1773) by his widow Eileen after his murder, tr. Frank O'Connor.

WHITMAN, *Leaves of Grass* (1891 edn.), 'Old War Dreams', 1st pub. 1865.

II SAMUEL (compiled from 960 BC), chapter 1, verses 17 and 19–24, Authorized Version of the Bible (1611), arranged as in *The Bible Designed to be Read as Literature*. King David lived *c*.1000 BC.

II SAMUEL, chapter 18, verses 32, 33 (as above).

SHAKESPEARE, *Antony and Cleopatra* (wr. 1607), act 4, scene 13.

MALORY, *Morte d'Arthur* (printed 1485), from 'The Dolorous death and departing out of this world of Sir Launcelot and Queen Guinevere'. Modernized.

ECCLESIASTICUS (*c.*180 BC), from chapter 44, Authorized Version of the Bible (1611), Apocrypha. (R.C. *Sirach.*)

CLARE, 'Memory' (wr. 1824–32).

WHITMAN, *Leaves of Grass* (1891 edn.), 'Song of Myself' (1st pub. 1855), part 18.

ALLINGHAM, 'No funeral gloom' (1890). No. 241 in *The New Oxford Book of Victorian Verse*, ed. Ricks (1987).

CHESTERTON, from 'Tommy and the Traditions', 1st pub. in the *Daily News*, 1908. *The Bodley Head G. K. Chesterton* (1985).

BRADSTREET, *Poems of Anne Bradstreet*, ed. Hutchinson (1969).

CRASHAW, *The Delight of the Muses* (1646).

RICHARDSON, 'On My Late Dear Wife' (wr. 1728), part 4. No. 128 in *The New Oxford Book of 18th Century Verse*, ed. Lonsdale (1984).

LEWIS, *A Grief Observed* (1961), from part 3.

JOHNSON, *The Rambler*, 1750, no. 48.

UNAMUNO, *The Tragic Sense of Life* (*Del Sentimiento Tràgico de la Vida*) (1912), tr. J. E. Crawford Flitch (1921), from chapter 11, 'The Practical Problem' (1964 edn.).

TOYNBEE, *End of a Journey, an autobiographical journal 1979–81* (1981), p.211.

Index of Authors